DISTANT VOICES

Contrasto®
is an editorial trademark of
© 2023 Roberto Koch Editore srl
Via Nizza, 56
00198 Roma
www.contrastobooks.com

Photographs © Steven Seidenberg
Texts © the authors

ISBN 9788869658969

DISTANT VOICES

ON STEVEN SEIDENBERG'S
ARCHITECTURE OF SILENCE

EDITED BY
CAROLYN L. WHITE

contrasto

TABLE OF CONTENTS

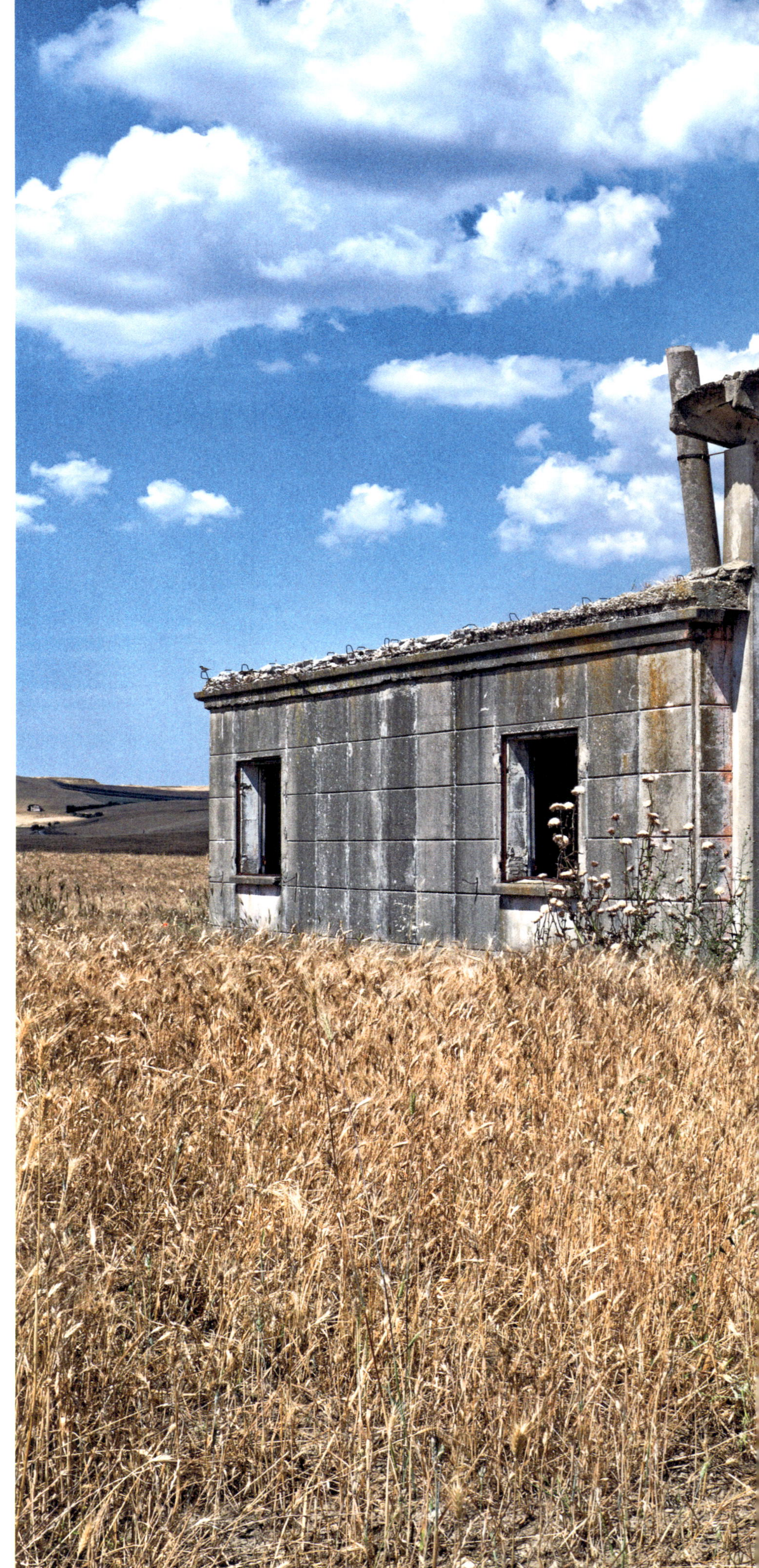

Figure 1

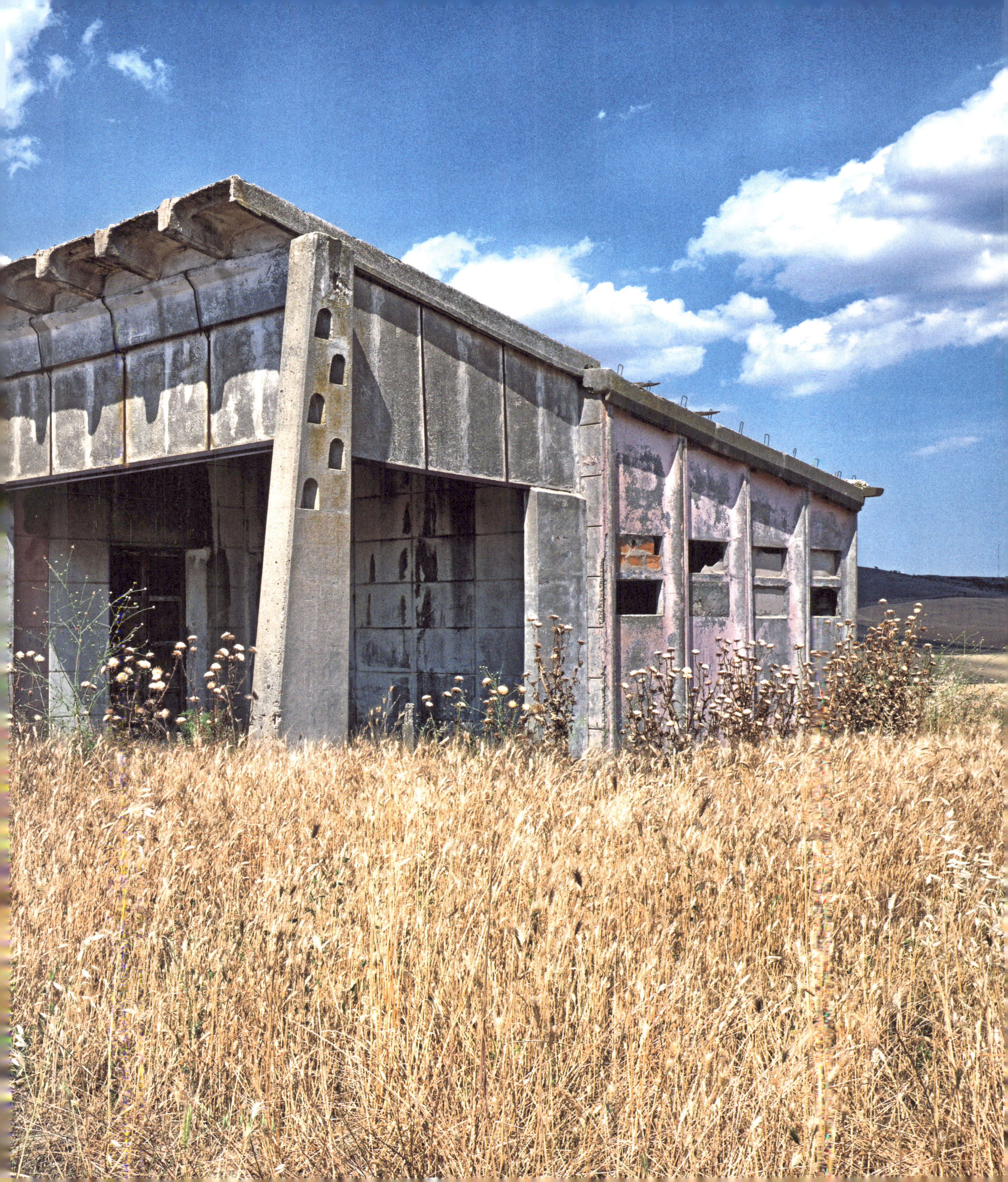

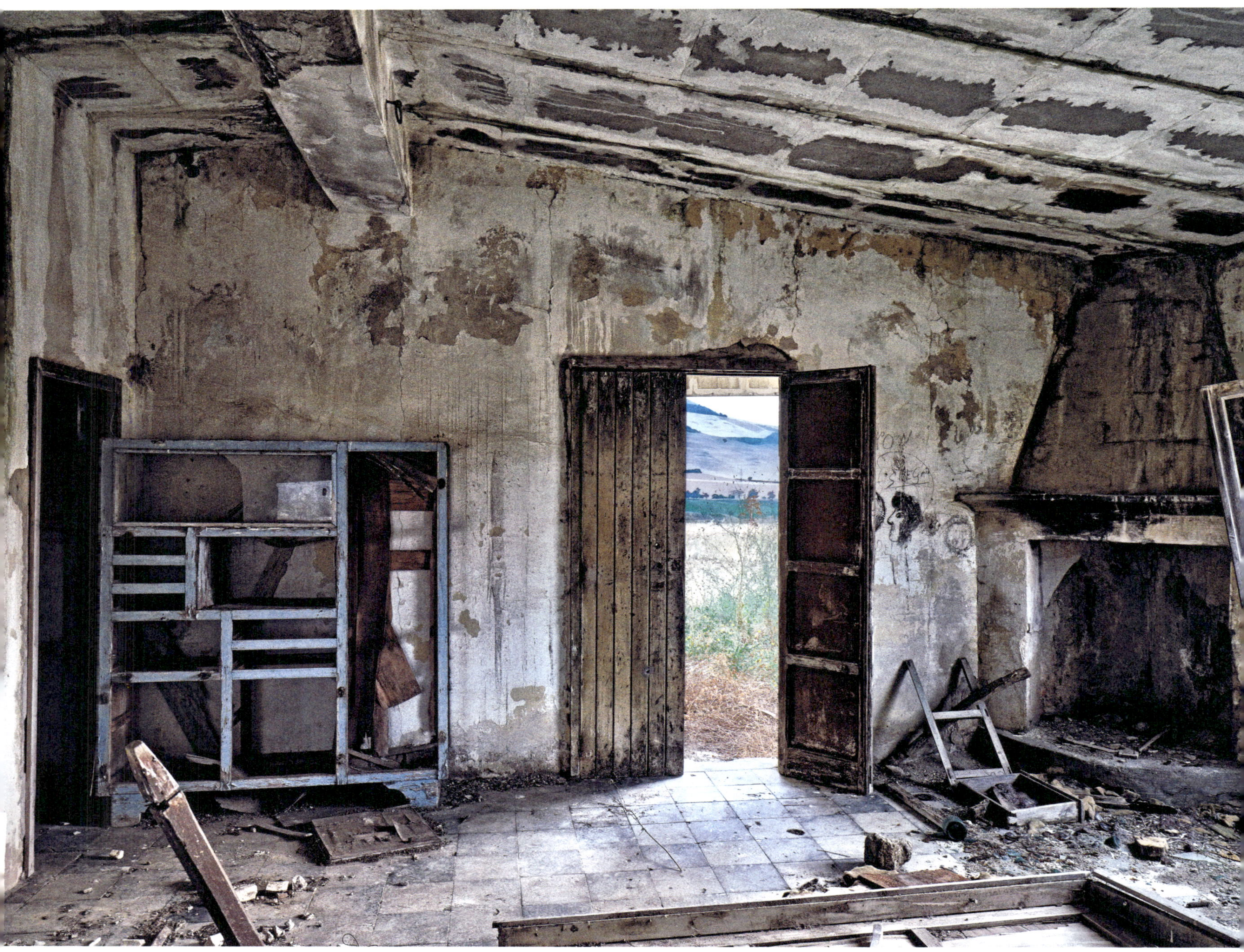

Figure 2

Steven Seidenberg's Photographs and *The Architecture of Silence*

As the Italian economy emerged from the ravages of World War II, the newly established republic and its American allies developed a program called the *Riforma Fondiaria*, a land reform measure designed to redistribute land to destitute peasants in several poor provinces. In addition to its declared purposes of breaking up large baronial estates and redistributing land to those in severe poverty, the program was motivated by the government's desire for a fast-working antidote to the rioting, unrest, and rise of the communist party in the south. Across the Italian landscape—predominantly in the south, but also in the Po River Valley—the program rezoned and redistributed land between 1950 to 1972 and its wake still curls through the fields today. Poorly planned and ineptly realized, the *Riforma Fondiaria* left lasting marks on the vast open plains photographed in *The Architecture of Silence*.

Two extensive reform laws authorized the dual purposes of subdividing large estates and reallocating the land to those in need.[1] Expropriations were made by Reform Authority boards (*Enti di Riforma*) licensed to calculate how much and from whom land could be reallocated in Basilicata and Puglia, based on per-hectare taxable income. Highly efficient and intensively used parcels of land were exempt; properties with the lowest yields were subject to the largest percentages of expropriation.[2] Eventually the provinces redistributed land to landless town inhabitants, sharecroppers, rural landless peasants, and farmers with dispersed or very limited land parcels, in that order of priority.[3] The new landholders obtained title for the land only after working it for two years (though without payments for three years) and they were forbidden to sell, rent, lease, or divide their properties for 30 years.[4]

1   Carlo Vanzetti and Frank Meissner, "The Agrarian Reform in Italy," *Land Economics* vol. 29 no. 2 (1953), 147.
2   Vanzetti and Meissner, 148-49.
3   Marco Percoro, "Land redistribution and local development: evidence from the Italian reform" (2014), 7; Vanzetti and Meissner, 150.
4   Contracts required annual payments over a 30-year term at 3.5% interest. Fees included compensation paid by the state to the original expropriated landholder plus two-thirds of the state's expenditures on improvements (Jim E. Davis, "New Hope in Italy: Land of the Noonday Sun," *Land Economics* vol. 35 no. 1 [1959], 61).

The Reform Authority promised basic improvements to the land with the intent of setting the new farmers up for success in their fresh endeavors. Each parcel of land was to include a house with attached stable, a cistern, two oxen, and—on a promise—electricity and connection to a municipal water supply. Further, the authority was supposed to build roads, houses, and outbuildings, install irrigation, drainage and potable well systems, and plant trees for shade and protection from the wind. There were to be programs to teach the formerly urban dwellers modern farming methods and schools to educate the children. Adjacent villages were built by the authorities to give the relocated smallholders a wider support network.[5]

Across some metrics, the program was a great success. By the end of 1956, more than half-a-million hectares had been distributed across Italy, and by 1972, 133,066 families had received allocations.[6] A promotional film from 1953 shows satisfied bureaucrats escorting cheerful peasants into their new homes, showing off modern amenities, spacious interiors, and optimistic attitudes.[7] In later years government reports hailed the program as successfully increasing yields across the region.

In reality, there were manifold problems and they came to the fore almost immediately. Most significantly, the size of the allocated parcels foretold failure. Because so many people qualified for the program, expropriated holdings were subdivided into allotments scaled for subsistence farming rather than the intended family-commercial farming. In Basilicata and Puglia parcels averaged 3 hectares per family (7.4 acres), far below the acreage needed for a family-commercial undertaking. The limited land meant that multiple crops could not be planted simultaneously, which would have allowed

5   Vanzetti and Meissner, 150; G. Gaetani D'Aragona, "A Critical Evaluation of Land Reform in Italy," *Land Economics* vol. 30, no. 1 (1954),16.
6   Total distribution was 578,649 hectares, although 740,000 had been expropriated (Davis, 63; these are the latest numbers reported in available sources). Of this, 208,572 hectares were in Basilicata and Puglia (D'Aragona, 16). It is not clear what happened to the remaining 161,351 hectares.
7   https://www.youtube.com/watch?v=_j3aBdxDXZc. Accessed January 31, 2021.

family labor to shift from field to field in an efficient cycle; instead, additional laborers had to be hired to accommodate bursts of activity as single crops matured.[8]

Other factors exacerbated the foundational flaw of parcel size and further augured the program's fate.[9] The more-than-anticipated numbers of participants meant that the budget was spent disproportionately on buildings, since each parcel required a farmhouse and associated outbuildings. Further, credit was in short supply, limiting farmers' abilities to buy supplies in advance of a successful harvest.[10] The very parameters of the program's land allocation strategy stacked the deck against the new farmers.[11] By law, the original landowners kept the highest-yielding portions of their property—the parcels allocated to the farmers were of poor quality, often suitable only for cereal crops. After the war the price of wheat was depressed severely, further challenging the farmers' path to financial solvency (average net income for the farmers was approximately $3000/€2600 annually in today's currency).[12] Irrigation never reached many of the farms, and land improvements fell short of what was promised. One contemporary observer commented that "the land expropriated in 99% of the cases lacks almost everything. There are no roads, no houses, no villages, no water, and, in short, it is without the basic elements needed to establish a settlement."[13] The residents moved into a place that was alien and uncomfortable when they relocated to the semi-isolated farms, far from the close-knit villages and towns they had known all of their lives. The privation was stark, and ultimately intolerable. One commentator described the conditions as "starvation, or something very similar to starvation. The result is that the peasants are starting to run away from the reform lands."[14]

8   D'Aragona, 17.
9   Vanzetti and Meissner, 151.
10 D'Aragona, 14.
11 Alessandro Bonanno, "Theories of the State: The Case of Land Reform in Italy, 1944-1961," *The Sociological Quarterly* vol. 29 no. 1 (1988), 140.
12 Bruno Leoni, "Economic Laws and Land Reform in Italy," *Il Politico* vol. 23 no. 4 (1958), 724.
13 M. Bandini, *La Riforma Fondiaria* (Rome: Edizione Cinque Lune, 1956), 54. Translated and quoted by Bonanno (1986), 140.
14 Leoni, 724.

Most of the new houses were abandoned within two years.[15]

In sum, the program "never created a stable network of small family farms for the landless peasants and farmworkers."[16] The limited yields and high costs of wheat production proved incapable of both supporting the families who occupied the *Riforma* houses and paying off the debt to the government accrued by their purchase.

Soon, the issues described found a labor force trapped in unsustainable conditions, needing more secure employment. When industry boomed in the north in 1958-1961, more than 3 million farmers filled a labor void as they went north to Lombardy to work in factories producing clothing, plastics, machinery, motor scooters, and cars.[17] The land, then, with loans defaulted and parcels abandoned, reverted to the state and was sold on, often to large agricultural interests, successfully transforming agricultural practice from the feudal to the corporate, increasing yields exponentially, but at the expense of those who effected the change.

Today, *Riforma* lands are mainly owned by corporations, including the pasta companies Barilla and DeCecco, who grow wheat, farro, and other grains on the still-unirrigated plains. Crops can be harvested by a single combine driver. The houses stand empty, though they are occasionally repurposed for storing minor supplies (fertilizer, tires, tarps), as shelters where combine drivers can have a nap, or as squatted or leased seasonal housing for migrant laborers, mostly from North Africa.

The Landscape Today

Built by the thousands not very long ago, and remaining in vast

15 C. Marciani, *L'esperienza di Riforma Agraria in Italia* (Rome: Giuffrè, 1966), 120; P. Pezzino, "The Agrarian Reform in Italy," *Monthly Review* vol. 8-9 [Italian edition, vol. 2-3), 1972, 120.
16 Bonnano, "Theories of the State," 141.
17 A Graziani, *L'Economia Italiana dal 1945 a Oggi*, 2d ed. (Bologna: Il Mulino, 1979),154; G. Mottura and E. Pugliese, *Agricoltura Mezzogiorno e Mercato del Lavoro* (Bologna: Il Mulino, 1975), 168; C. Podbielski, *Italy: Development and Crisis in the Post- War Economy* (Oxford: Clarendon Press, 1974),15; Bonnano, "Theories of the State," 142.

numbers today, very little is known about the construction, form, or life within the structures built by the *Riforma*. My work alongside Seidenberg's has surveyed and recorded the buildings as a means to envision what life was like for the inhabitants of the buildings, towns, dispersed settlements during this time. While it is common to hear from residents of nearby villages that the program was a failure and "no one lived in the houses" it is clear from visiting them that they were abodes for settlement—temporary yes, and often abandoned quickly—inhabited by people, by families. The materiality of the structures reflects those occupations.

The houses are made in several different styles, some in cast concrete hyper-modernism, while others seem modelled on suburban split level homes, made of brick and concrete block. There are hybrid forms and additions and reworkings of the parts—slightly different floor plans, interchangeable components in the facades, a mix and match of pieces found elsewhere. While repetitive, there is endless variation.

In one image, Seidenberg presents a three-quarter view of a cast concrete house (Figure 1). Placed against the summer sky and rising from the wheat, the house is uncanny and forbidding. The steeply pitched wedge of a roof covers an exterior portico, the shadowed door beneath open to the viewer. The broken windows and streaks of decay on the concrete slabs reveal its age, even as the architectural form projects an anachronistic futurism. So Seidenberg immediately pushes into the historical contradiction this series recovers from dissemblance—an optimism of policy and design that is structurally, *essentially* undermined by incompetent planning, unattainable goals, and a lack of understanding of the alienation the displaced families would feel. Other exteriors are similarly framed against open fields and skies, a seemingly idyllic landscape filled with deserted relics of families, displaced from one liminal life for the hope of a better one. In one image we see two identical buildings sited some distance from a dirt track, surrounded by overgrown wheat. Seidenberg's framing reinforces their isolation.

Inside the Buildings

So far, the only description of the buildings' interiors comes from a 1958 government publication that describes Po Valley farms in which every farmer was "settled in a home built on his own piece of land. Each dwelling was provided with a good size living room, a kitchen, two bedrooms, a storeroom, an indoor lavatory with tub or shower. Built in proximity of each house was a stall for three to four animals, a pigsty, a hen house, and a small silo." Archaeological survey in Basilicata and Puglia supports this basic form—the houses consistently have a living room, kitchen, two bedrooms, storeroom, and an attached stall for animals, but the basic description actually covers a far ranging set of exteriors and interiors.

The pamphlet suggests a standard form, but Seidenberg's photographs reveal the gap between the rather sanguine description and the reality of what can be found in the fields, of the abundant variability within that repetition. Each house does contain a living room/kitchen, two bedrooms, a storeroom, and an indoor lavatory, but they lack tubs or showers. The promised electricity is irregular and makeshift. The stalls that housed livestock are attached to the buildings, but access to them appears to have been an afterthought—unfinished doors are chopped through an interior wall.

From a distance many houses look stalwart and inhabitable, seemingly in need of a mere cosmetic refresh, but the insides convey the passage of time. Spare, cold, and gloomy, the interiors maintain very basic decorations of tinted plaster walls in pale blues and pinks, checkerboard floor tiling, and hooks, wires, and poles that supplied storage for the occupants' things. Mattresses lie on the floor, springs and metal frames emerging like skeletons from decomposing carcasses of ticking and filling. A cushionless couch stands near a half open balcony egress, fractured glass and splintered shutters framing the view of distant fields and hills (cover photo). Garments left by the original inhabitants erode on the floor, mingled with their collapsed clothes rack and fractured hangers.

Seidenberg shows a central room with its furnishings in situ, but crumbling, shot to capture the ceiling, floor, and walls and providing a sense of the volume of the space. A smashed chair lies beside the fireplace, the bones of a massive cabinet stand against a wall (Figure 2). A doorframe lies across the picture's foreground. We can imagine the space in use, almost as much as we can imagine the passage of time since its use.

By dint of Seidenberg's manipulation of focal length and depth of field, other interior images take on the flat quality of a painting, the shadows intertwined with the dusky staining of the walls to form a photographic chiaroscuro. In one, the soot-softened red walls are stamped with vestiges of furnishings (Figure 3). A soapstone sink stands beside a stove, rusted nails beneath the ghostly outlines of missing shelves. Above it all, a piece of the stovepipe chimney descends from the ceiling, and a large white and black stain traces the former connection down to the stove. Doors frame the scene, one distinguished by the addition of a charcoaled portrait; the other gapes open. The graffito of decay seems composed scratched into the walls as though with intent.

Steven Seidenberg's photographic project of the landscapes and houses of the *Riforma Fondiaria* limns remains of the post-World War II land reform movement in southern Italy. His photographic crossings of the wheat fields between Matera in Basilicata and Altamura in Puglia relate the place of the structures in the landscape, their contents, and their present reuse as both storage for agricultural supplies and occasional housing for migrant farm workers, mostly from North Africa. The images function as both formal renderings that stress color, tone, and texture—discursively related to other portrayals of the desolate and the abandoned, both technically and compositionally—and as documentation of the material devastation of those whose lives in this place have left no other point of access in the contemporary world. Despite claims that "no one lived there," Seidenberg's work makes it clear that people did.

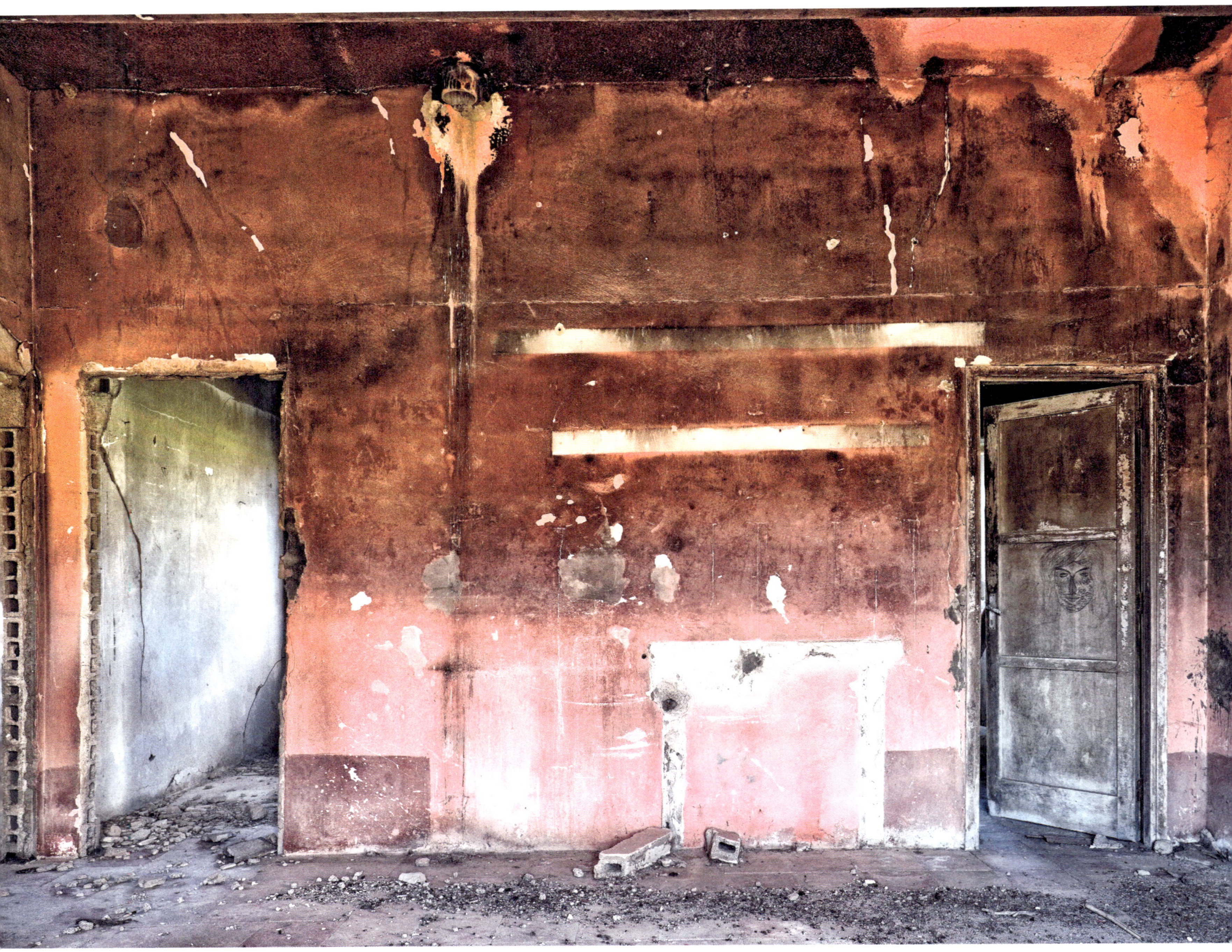

Figure 3

PETER KALB

The Provocation of the Unpopulated Landscape

Unpopulated landscapes are always about the people who left and those who may appear. At both ends of the history of photography, from the gentle lake views of Fox Talbot, the great survey photographs of Timothy O'Sullivan and Eadward Muybridge, and the celebrations of Yosemite by Carlton Watkins, to the extremist panoramas of Thomas Joshua Cooper and the rigor of Bernd and Hilla Becher and their Dusseldorf students, images of a world bereft of people rebuke the fantasy of untouched terrain. These are landscapes in the process of being marked by class, mapped by the state, extracted by capital, and curiously, compassionately, and perhaps even insidiously crafted into visions of sublime and poignant beauty. Photographs of empty streets, vacated homes, and unpeopled terrain are ethical provocations aimed at our understanding of the past and the present.

The history of photography famously began with an unpopulated cityscape: Joseph Nicéphore Niépce's view out his window at Le Gras in 1827. With that image, Niépce not only advanced photographic technology, he created a genre. In a few short decades the photographic archive filled with scenes of empty streets from Paris to Cairo to Arizona. Though certainly begun as a function of the technology, the subsequent history of unpopulated cityscapes testifies to the need such empty scenes satisfied. The genre facilitated a form of archaeology directed at the Ancient, Medieval, and Modern world alike. Forgoing the shovel for the lens, daguerreotypists took the first step, collecting images of the Greek and Roman cities the way their more material bound colleagues brought back marbles. They were followed by those practicing every new form of photography, many of whom eagerly turned their tools from the sites of the past to the spaces of the present. This mode of photographic archaeology lent the genre a unique form of temporal dualism that would be echoed in the narratives such photos told and their character as photographs.

Look at empty Paris: After Niépce, the photographs of Charles Marville in the 1850s and Eugene Atget by the turn of the century set upon the spaces of daily life to capture, in the first case, moments in the flux of Parisian history and, in the second, the curiosity of Paris as a public space. Taken together they are evidence of an analytical gaze unprecedented in the history of art that generated an archive of past and present with no clear allegorical, theological, or moral intent. The medieval street likely to be displaced by the Haussmann's Boulevard or the black suit to be purchased by the bourgeoisie appear before us without distinction, each claiming equal import and equal attention from the viewer. This disinterested view, one begun with Baudelaire and ending with Breton, would fuse the historical moment that birthed the photograph's subject matter with the instant of the photograph and the experience of the image. The material world, captured without its human hosts, was adrift between the historical and contemporary, at once either, both, and neither.

In the streets of Paris, European audiences could distinguish the history implied by the photography of Old Paris from the style of bourgeois home; hence the provocation of subjecting them both to the scrutiny of the photographer/archaeologist. Similar contrasts abroad created very different effects. Photographs of Egyptian temples and empty Cairo streets were unmoored from an understanding of history; in such images the future took priority. Not only did the genre facilitate an ahistorical analysis of the object at hand, but it invited viewers to project any form of life back into these vacated spaces. Onto Francis Frith's empty Egyptian streets arrive European soldiers; into the archaic Navajo settlements documented by O'Sullivan come White settlers; through Atget's Paris walk Surrealist explorers. By the 1920s, modernist visions of sky-scraped metropolises propose citizens suited for an idealized mechanistic future and more recently the early morning that stills Thomas Struth's German streets or Catherine Opie's LA malls will be peopled by a diversity of residents. While the archaeological nature of the depopulated landscape links the past and present, the narrative of return invites us to consider the future.

It is, of course, a common refrain regarding photography that it is defined by its simultaneous and perpetual existence in the moment of its production and the time its reception. When we look at a photograph, we are, as Roland Barthes points out, invited into a triangulated relationship with the photographer as they opened the shutter, the subject imbedded in its own history, and ourselves viewing the resulting image[1]. Thus the narrative past and futures of the scene intertwine with the ontological past and futures of the photographic object, leaving the viewer faced with a complex web of unresolved positions. Each emptied image, from Niépce's forward, is a proposal to consider the fixed conditions of creation in dialog and often in dispute with the complexities of an ever changing present. At this point, it is the genre itself, by invoking the archaeological gaze, the narratives of evacuation and repopulation, and by simply being a photograph that satisfies the first part of Hubert Damisch's proposition that "Photography aspires to art each time, in practice, it calls into question its essence and its historical roles."[2]

If the unpopulated landscape cannot fail to represent its missing population, it likewise points to the space beyond its frame to reconcile its moral and ethical provocation and satisfies Damisch's second point, that as art, photography must also "[uncover] the contingent character of these things…"[3] In the first place, the narrative of evacuation and return necessarily incorporates life outside the picture. Seidenberg can take his photographs because historical forces have emptied these homes. In contrast, photographers such as Niépce or digital photographers over a century later count on technology to clear the space, while others simply wait for the right time of day. Together with the archaeological and futurological nature of the genre, the logistics of taking the photo draw our attention to a complex and ambiguous network of history, technology, power and time that necessarily invokes far more than can be seen in the photograph.

1 Roland Barthes, *Camera Lucida: Reflections on Photography* (1st American ed. New York: Hill and Wang, 1981).
2 Hubert Damisch, "Five Notes for a Phenomenology of the Photographic Image," *October* Vol. 5, Photography (Summer, 1978), pp. 70-72.
3 *Ibid*, 72.

In the face of the temporal and moral gymnastics performed by unpopulated landscape imagery, photographers have reached beyond the frame to guide their viewers. Ideologies of progress, state support, journalism, religion, and economic interests are all strong forces orienting the networks of power often invisible in these photographs. Thus, one turns to oeuvres rather than single photographs for understanding. Comparing, for instance, Watkins's sublime images of the vistas of the California wilderness with his scenes of hydraulic mining that was turning mountains into gravel, might trouble our understanding of the artist, but it clarifies the status of the image. Modernists helped explain their "cubistic" vistas, as critics called them, by taking their viewers from the towering skyscrapers to architectural proposals for a new society or to kindred forms rooted in rural spaces far from the modern city. Catherine Opie provides one of the most elegant resolutions to the question of ethics in landscape photography by surrounding the images of banal LA with a diverse portrait of the lives that awaken within it. In these cases, the viewer might not always like what their artist-guides propose, but they can find direction in the art itself.

In some cases, the answers lie outside the art, proposing an answer to how we might react to provocation outside the museum. Niépce's image set the stage and not just metaphorically. The appeal of the empty city, especially one constructed with abstract geometric forms, can be seen in stage design of the early twentieth century, particularly in the work of the Russian Constructivists or Expressionist film makers. Even before photographic technology could be enlisted to occupy the stage itself, the idea that photography was a means of thinking theater in two dimensions had taken hold. The heavily populated and melodramatic composite photography by Oscar Rejlander or Henry Peach Robinson implies in their processes the empty stage set for the cast of characters that will be added to it. Contemporary set-designer and photographer, Marsha Ginsburg's images of abandoned Catskill hotels and bungalow colonies is an exemplary instance of unpopulated photographs existing to provoke further work for the theater. The empty room like the empty street and the empty stage is a starting point for other creators, even the viewer, to tell their stories and thus accomplishes Damisch's final requirement, "Soliciting in us the producer rather than the consumer of images."[4]

The invitation to act that is prompted by the unpopulated photographic landscapes extends well beyond the arts. In the legacy of Social Work Photography of the turn of the century, Walker Evans photographed the neat corner of a Hale County, Alabama farmhouse to provoke his viewers to contribute money to sustaining poor communities in the south. The vast landscape images of Subhankar Banerjee are created and contextualized to inspire action outside the museum or the studio. Both artists enveloped their artistic practice with political action. We may find ethical guidance to working our way into and through Seidenberg's southern Italian landscape by looking at what he is doing when he is not taking photographs, and what we are doing when we are not looking at them.

4   *Ibid*, 72.

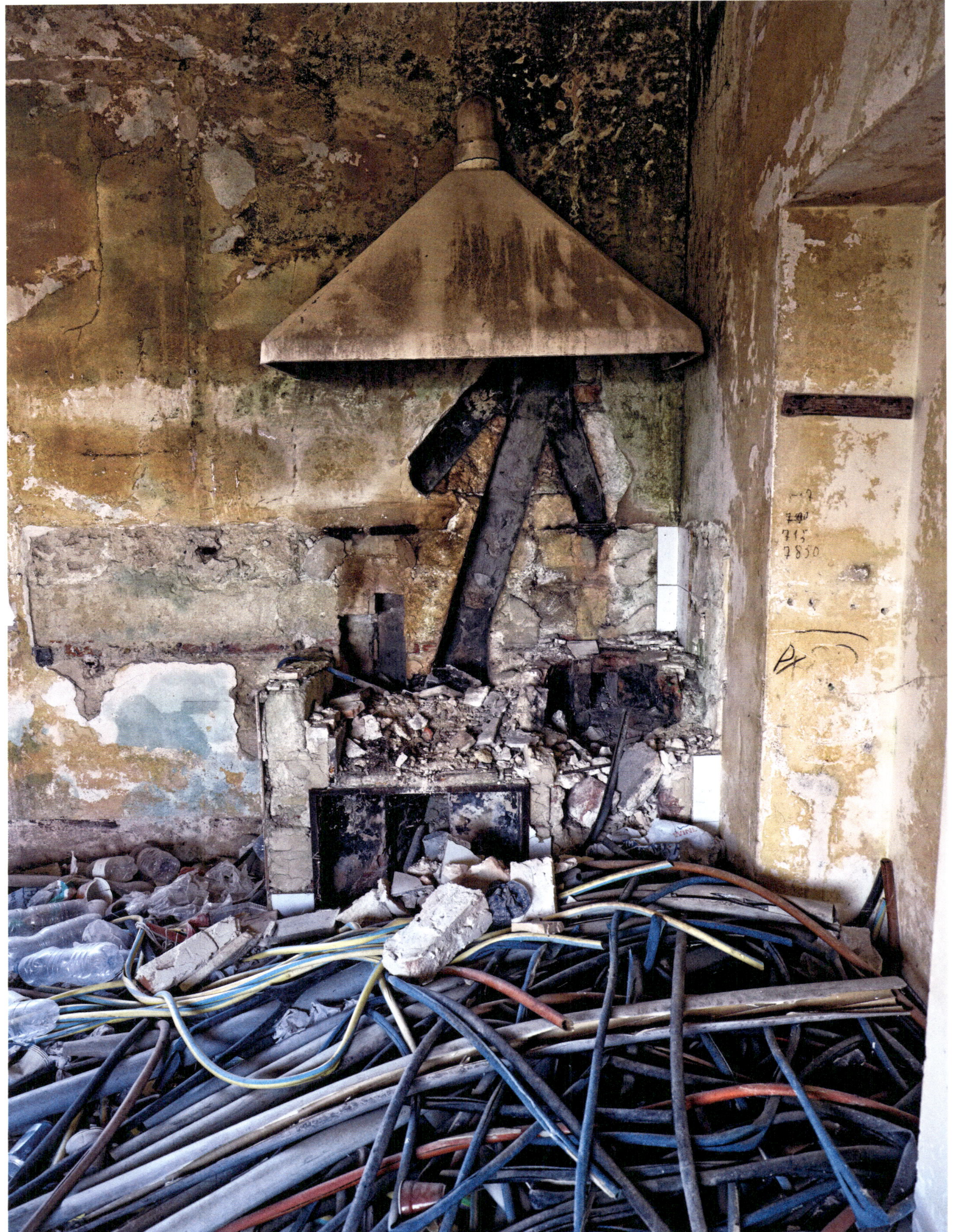

Figure 4

SAVERIO MASSARO

**Learning from *Riforma*'s Failure:
Three Open Questions about the *Riforma
Agraria*'s Legacy**

The *Riforma Agraria* is one of the great Italian reforms that has not been implemented. It is a failed attempt, as highlighted by the authors of this volume, and also a great betrayal, particularly for Southern Italy. At such distance in time, what legacy does this experience leave us? But above all, what lessons can be learned from unfinished business and failure?

I reflect on three open questions that outline and contextualize the actions of Seidenberg and his collaborators, paying particular attention to the territory of Alta Murgia.

The investigation carried out by Seidenberg, White, and McCallum[1] joins the array of research on the Alta Murgia area that spans from the 1990s to the present day focused on the phenomenon and the traces of rural society. For example, the Centro Studi Torre di Nebbia[2] focuses on natural and anthropic perspectives on the Alta Murgia, and Ferdinando Mirizzi dedicated much of his research to rural settlement forms and the history of the material culture of the societies of Southern Italy, with particular reference to the Apulian-Lucan territories. Since his first book *Tra la fossa e le lame. Territorio, insediamenti, cultura materiale nell'alta Murgia* (Congedo, 1990) to his most recent work, he described the relationship between urban development and rural society, deepening the spatial and functional characteristics of the houses.

More recently, the architect-photographer Sante Cutecchia has used photography, like Seidenberg, to capture the continuing aesthetic value of the architectural traces of rural civilization located in the urban fabric of Altamura. In his book *La città di mezzo* (Esperidi, 2015)

1   Carolyn L. White, Steven Seidenberg, and Myles McCallum, "Disaster for the People, Bonanza for the State," *Places Journal*, September 2019. https://doi.org/10.22269/190903. Accessed April 27, 2020.
2   The Torre di Nebbia Study Centre was founded in 1988 in Altamura and is a permanent observatory for the recognition, protection, and enhancement of the human and environmental heritage of the Alta Murgia territory. Source: http://www.altramurgia.it/il-centro-studi-di-torre-di-nebbia.html.

Cutecchia explores the slow and inexorable process of compromise and disappearance of rural dwellings, urban and historical vestiges abandoned to themselves and increasingly swallowed up by new building typologies through photography.

The urban peasants' dwellings and the reform's houses in the countryside today share the same alienating condition of isolation, as decontextualized entities. Seidenberg's photography reveals the impossibility of the areas and artifacts to be fully configured as a landscape and at the same time highlights the "detachment" of which the agrarian reform is the emblem.

The disconnection, primarily in terms of vision and political action, is highlighted by the historian Raffaele De Leo[3], who states:

> An overall reading of the action carried out by the Authority – here only briefly exemplified – highlights the asymmetry between the multiplicity of initiatives, investments and realizations in the field of transformation cooperation and the poverty of results in the field of structural policies, i.e., policies that should support and strengthen the productive base on which peasant enterprises gathered in cooperatives are based. This asymmetry appears even more evident if we underline the lack of activation of some experiences that in other European countries were considered as an effective tool of land policy, i.e., the associated conductions.

The decision to fragment rather than associate is therefore the first element that reveals a complete misalignment between tools and methods used related to the goals pursued. Without sharing there can be no landscape. Therefore it's quite difficult to define a "landscape of reform" because it remains fundamentally unimplemented due to a lack of sharing and co-creation between the different actors involved. The idea of reform remains a lifeless zoning that has left mute skeletons and has not produced any reorganization

3   Raffaele De Leo, "The difficult transition from land reform to development policies. Observations starting from the Puglia-Lucania-Molise case," in AA.VV., *Land Reform and Landscape*, Rubbettino, 2011, 13.

or decentralization of power, as was hoped. Seidenberg's images succeed in capturing the distance between the expected and the unfulfilled and they represent the betrayal of a disregarded idea of landscape.

What, then, is the legacy of the reforms today?

Seidenberg's photographs tell a cross-section of what Rossi Doria defines as "Mezzogiorno nudo" (naked South), whose main characteristics are extensive agriculture, the cereal-pastoral economy, and landownership,[4] as well as "naked architectural traces of the reform, the uninhabited houses that turn into sounding boxes of a deafening silence, a void of relationships, the perennial lack of care and vision." An integral part of this heritage is also the cultural heritage made up of all those archives (photos, videos, documents, etc.) that collate the memories, testimonies, and knowledge of the agriculturalists and testify to the clashes, social struggles and protests that have taken place over the years.

Not least, the reform leaves a legacy of errors of method and approach; it provided for the allocation of about one hectare to a farming family, but without agricultural means, seeds, access to credit, and resources for the marketing of products.[5] The recognition of these errors suggests a second question.

What framework and strategies to suggest?

The documents presented to the Constituent of the Earth (1947)[6] make clear that the reorganization of agriculture was one of the most important requirements for democratic reconstruction. Rossi Doria defines the agrarian reform as a "peace policy, anti-imperi-

4   Manlio Rossi Doria, *Riforma agraria e azione meridionalista* (Bologna, Edizioni Agricole, 1948), 5.
5   Alfonso Gianni and Tonino Perna, "Ci vuole una seconda riforma agraria". Available at: https://www.che-fare.com/ci-vuole-una-seconda-riforma-agraria/
6   Comitato d'iniziativa per la costituente della terra, Documenti presentati alla Costituente della Terra, Bologna 21 dicembre 1947, Stabilimento tipografico U.E.S.I.S.A., Roma.

alist, anti-protectionist, decentralizing, aimed at ensuring freedom of trade, freedom of emigration, training of savings, tax justice."[7] Time has shown that the reform has been nothing more than a signifier of top-down policies that has been dropped from the top in a homogeneous way, without taking into account the specificities of each territory or considering the ways and means of what we would call today *empowerment,* in order to lift agrarian people out of their impoverished condition.

The reform's territories lie in the "inner areas"[8] that are subject to exponential phenomena such as impoverishment and depopulation, and to which the National Strategy of Internal Areas (SNAI; launched in 2013) tries to respond. It is an example of a *place-based* policy using Community-Led Local Development principles that finds its roots and driving force in field practice, in the mending of frayed communities and relationships, to propose scenarios of change and improvement in terms of infrastructure, services, and welfare.

The work of SNAI makes clear that the fate of agricultural areas is linked to that of small municipalities in inland areas, since many of these realities "imagine their future by linking it to a revival of the combination of agriculture and tourism, placing the restoration of the landscape as a synthesis of local culture at the center."[9]

7   Rossi Doria, 2.
8   "Italy's 'inner areas' are rural areas characterised by their distance from the main service centres (education, health and mobility). [...] The demographic and agricultural profile of Inner Areas is notably different form the average profile emerging at the national level. [...] Demographic decline and population ageing is more pronounced in Inner Areas than in the rest of Italy [...]. Farm abandonment and unused land is also a bigger issue in Inner Areas, due to lower land productivity in these areas. Economic productivity and the quality of services in these areas is also affected by the digital divide. Despite these negative characteristics, Inner Areas still contain important environmental resources (water, high-quality agricultural products, forests, natural and human landscapes) and cultural assets (archaeological, historic settlements, abbeys, small museums, skills centres). They are also extremely diversified, as the result of their varied natural systems, and centuries' old settlement processes." Source: enrd.ec.europa.eu
9   Ministry for Territorial Cohesion and the South, Annual Report on the National Strategy for Domestic Areas, 2016, 4.

What can art contribute?

In Italy there is longstanding and continuing discussion about the recovery and reuse of existing heritage, the vastness in quantitative terms and the impossibility recovering it entirely. The legacy of the reform is an emblem of this impossibility. But what *Imaging Failure* conveys is not the idea of recovering existing artifacts *tout court*, since it highlights the abandonment of entire areas and vast portions of territory that are the result of the abandonment of policies and disregarded visions. The photographs go far beyond the fate of individual artifacts and their essentiality. *The Architecture of Silence,* then, reminds us of the need to go back and redesign networks of relations and reformulate common and collective objectives, in the light of the strong complexities and contradictions that contemporary reality proposes. These are the premises for formulating an idea of landscape from the reform's legacy.

Ultimately, *The Architecture of Silence* reflects on the concept of "rural" in the first two decades of the 21st century. In the urban era, marked by the urbanization of more than half of the world's population by 2050, one wonders what the condition and fate of rural areas outside the cities might be. Far from a bucolic vision, today the "rural" is the object of a new and growing attention, as demonstrated by the recent exhibition *Countryside, The Future*[10] at the Guggenheim Museum in New York. The rural is a field of experimentation into which pours what cities produce, imagine, or cannot absorb.

In this sense, art can play a pivotal role in the formulation of a new narrative linked to the *countryside* and the return to the land. In the globalized world, the role of the earth becomes central again, but in a strongly changed context. Today the return to the earth no longer derives only from economic reasons or subsistence needs, but it is increasingly the result of more demanding life expectations. Thus, the land regains its role as a producer of cultural values, capable of

10 The exhibition addresses urgent environmental, political, and socioeconomic issues through the lens of architect and urbanist Rem Koolhaas and Samir Bantal, Director of AMO, the thinktank of the Office for Metropolitan Architecture (OMA).

activating pieces of society interested in different ways of production and consumption.

In the margin of these open-ended questions, Seidenberg and his collaborators look-action prompt me to share two further considerations. First of all, their investigation, accompanied by artistic practice, is not limited to the pure representation of what is there, but provides a lens through which to understand and, at the same time, redesign the present. Or perhaps better, it seems to suggest what the Italian philosopher Giorgio Agamben would call a "project for the past", whereby the past is made up of a stratification of infinite "unfinished" and the aim of the contemporary project is to turn our gaze to the past to try to complete the unfinished.

Seidenberg takes a look at the traces of the 1950s and 1960s that is not nostalgic, but rather captures the fractures, the interruptions, the cracks, and the collapses from which it is appropriate to contemplate a new start of an intervention that was never fully implemented, but whose realization seems to be more necessary today than ever. This volume is an invitation to strengthen the attention, civil commitment, and planning capacity that a territory can express, imagining itineraries of meaning capable of repositioning the traces of agrarian reform in the contemporary world. I hope that the three questions I propose will be a stimulus to confront each other and imagine possible answers together.

Pressed Against It

"First of all, on the surface on which I am going to paint, I draw a rectangle of whatever size I want," writes Leon Battista Alberti in his treatise *On Painting*, composed in 1435. This enframed flatness-within-a-flatness, Alberti continues, "I regard as an open window through which the subject to be painted is seen."[1]

It's a famous passage, suggesting complicated things about perception and imagination, and the fact that pictures must end at their borders while our dense actual surroundings don't or can't. The Renaissance polymath is offering a verbal image about visual images, in which a depthless opening-through-which-to-see is laid out across a planar piece of material, the pictorial support (which in 15th century Italy was likely to have been a wood panel). As the art historian Joseph Masheck explains, Alberti invites us to imagine that we can see through solid matter, a metaphor for the fantasies involved in making art: "The flat surface with edges precedes what Alberti calls a window, which is a construct, willfully imposed. The 'window' idea, then, is a trope, and a signal of the essentially fictive poetics of painting."[2]

Steven Seidenberg is a photographer, not a painter (also a poet, musician, and trained philosopher; i.e., a polymath) and not all his photographs of abandoned *Riforma Fondiaria* housing in southern Italy include windows or doorways. But most do—and even those in which unbroken surfaces are framed head-on draw the viewer's attention to marks on walls or detritus on floors that rhyme with the windows and doors we know must be just out of frame. A rectangular brown stain high on a graffitied wall neatly meets the seam between the wall and ceiling, as if the splotch were structural to the

1   Leon Battista Alberti, *On Painting and On Sculpture*, trans. Cecil Grayson (London: Phaidon, 1972), 55. Quoted in Julia Ordell, "Window" (2003) in the "Keywords" resource of the Chicago School of Media Theory at the University of Chicago. https://lucian.uchicago.edu/blogs/mediatheory/keywords/window/. Accessed January 23, 2020.
2   Joseph Masheck, "Alberti's 'Window': Art-Historiographic Notes on an Antimodernist Misprision," *Art Journal*, Vol. 50, No. 1, (Spring 1991), 35. https://www.jstor.org/stable/777083. Accessed January 24, 2020.

architecture; the bloody splash of paint below this window-sized stain has dripped to the baseboard but not below it, emphasizing differences in depth between the wall, the baseboard, and the floor. A tangle of discarded blue and red plastic pipes surrounds a metal-framed concrete box that must have been the house's built-in wood oven; a group of openings embedded in the wall (channels for the smoke) point like an arrow to the chimney itself, an exit portal (Figure 4). A pair of broken tvs piled one on top of the other suggest blocked conduits to the faraway—and the dull gray, slightly convex screen of the upper one reflects, in miniature, another oven-box and a window-hole filled with bright blue sky (Figure 5). True, the inner components of the bottom tv are gone, and its plastic cabinet is stuffed with trash—and in the photograph of another dead but slightly updated television or computer monitor, the promise of connection to images that come from beyond the room, beyond the house, beyond the village of Santa Maria Di Irsi, is both asserted and denied by the chunk of concrete sitting in the middle of the dusty screen face-up on the floor (Figure 6). If the concrete block had fallen there, it would have cracked the glass. So someone placed it—some bored joker or sculptural arranger of mundane stuff, a force of intentionality hinted at, as well, by the plastic stool drawn up awkwardly close to the monitor-and-rock array.

In Seidenberg's exterior photographs, we see the expanses of luscious bleakness in which the *Riforma* houses stand. Moody skies roil above ochre fields in Basilicata and Puglia, the tips of the tall grasses dramatically backlit. The days glow, though dappled with big clouds, and it looks windy; by contrast, the brick-and-concrete hulks are dark inside, their glassless window cut-outs and doorless doorways punctuating the rugged landscapes with repeating rectilinear black voids (Figure 7). At least one house still has its shutters. Yet even these flattened surfaces, accentuating the building's openings by closing them, reiterate the layering of one space into another that attracts Seidenberg's eye.

These apertures in built space—and the screens and stains that mimic them—are not "fictive" or "poetic" in Masheck's sense. They are not invented. This is a documentary project, in which the photographer collaborated with archaeologists to map the remnants of material culture left behind by participants in a failed postwar scheme for national land reform. The economic and political history of the *Riforma Fondiaria* is important; the Italian state appropriated properties from large landowners, and later sold them at a profit when the smallholders who had been allocated land in underpopulated areas defaulted on their government-sponsored loans. But one doesn't have to know this history to understand what the photographs make clear, which is that the cost in effort—by the workers who built the buildings, the farming families who were meant to inhabit them, and the migrant laborers who sometimes now squat there—has been grindingly real. When Seidenberg shows us daylight pouring through a bunker-like gray-and-white apartment, or lets us glimpse a vertical slice of countryside through a wooden door left ajar, he isn't fabricating scenes or pretending to see through walls (or photographic paper). He isn't "drawing a rectangle of whatever size he wants," but recording the physical facts of places where people tried to establish livelihoods, and couldn't, and eventually gave up and moved away.

The *Riforma* sites at Irsina and Santa Maria Di Irsi are real, and Seidenberg doesn't want us to think they aren't; lumpy mattresses on the floor and clothes abandoned on a makeshift clothesline stand in for the embodied presences of people who have used these rooms, just as the televisions stand for their imaginative vitality, their dream-lives (Figure 8). At the same time, nonetheless, we are encouraged to read the photographs as painterly constructs, in which tropes that go back to Alberti, regulating the composition of landscapes and interiors, remain potent. A dirt road plunges back from the picture plane, establishing a sharp orthogonal. The sliver of country seen through the half-open door looks like the background in a Fra Angelico, its blue mountains receding to fresco-like softness, its vegetation a surprising shade of hazy malachite. A squarish window in a mauve-pink room is photographed so that the frames of its broken panes, splayed against the inside wall, further overdetermine the framing-within-framing of the dry gold grass outside, the low hill in the distance patched with cultivated fields, and the sky with its pale clouds—shapes recapitulated in the blotches of rotten plaster on the water-damaged wall under the window (Figure 9).

All this is to say that—as tender and curious as he is about the lives people have led for decades in these dwellings, and as thoughtful as he is about the ways in which wind and heat and damp and cold eat up a building that's left empty—Seidenberg remains a formalist. He loves the architectonic order of a tightly composed shot; the classical rigor of stacking foreground and midground against horizon; the ancient chance-operation of discerning wonders in blemished walls and mineral striations.[3] He relishes the saturated, half-exhausted color furnished for his camera by the Italian summer and the long-ago décor choices of *Riforma* residents. He's a formalist—but not a purely optical thinker about image-making. He gravitates to geometric relations and repeated forms nested in the bounded space of the constructed image. But as a student of the visceral traces of human use in the built environment, he seems to want to touch everything he looks at—its jaggedness and grit, its dust and mildew, its breeziness and powdery fragility, its twisted cloth and scored concrete and splintered wood, its tile floor split by the intrusion of a vigorously healthy young fig tree. He makes us feel as if we're pressed against it.

3   "By looking attentively at old and smeared walls, or stones and veined marble of various colours, you may fancy that you see in them several compositions, landscapes, battles, figures in quick motion, strange countenances, and dresses, with an infinity of other objects. By these confused lines the inventive genius is excited to new exertions." *A Treatise on Painting*, chapter CLXIII, attributed to Leonardo da Vinci, trans. John Francis Rigaud, Esq. (London: J.B. Nichols and Son, 1835), 84. https://archive.org/stream/davincionpainting00leon/davincionpainting00leon_djvu.txt. Accessed January 23, 2020.

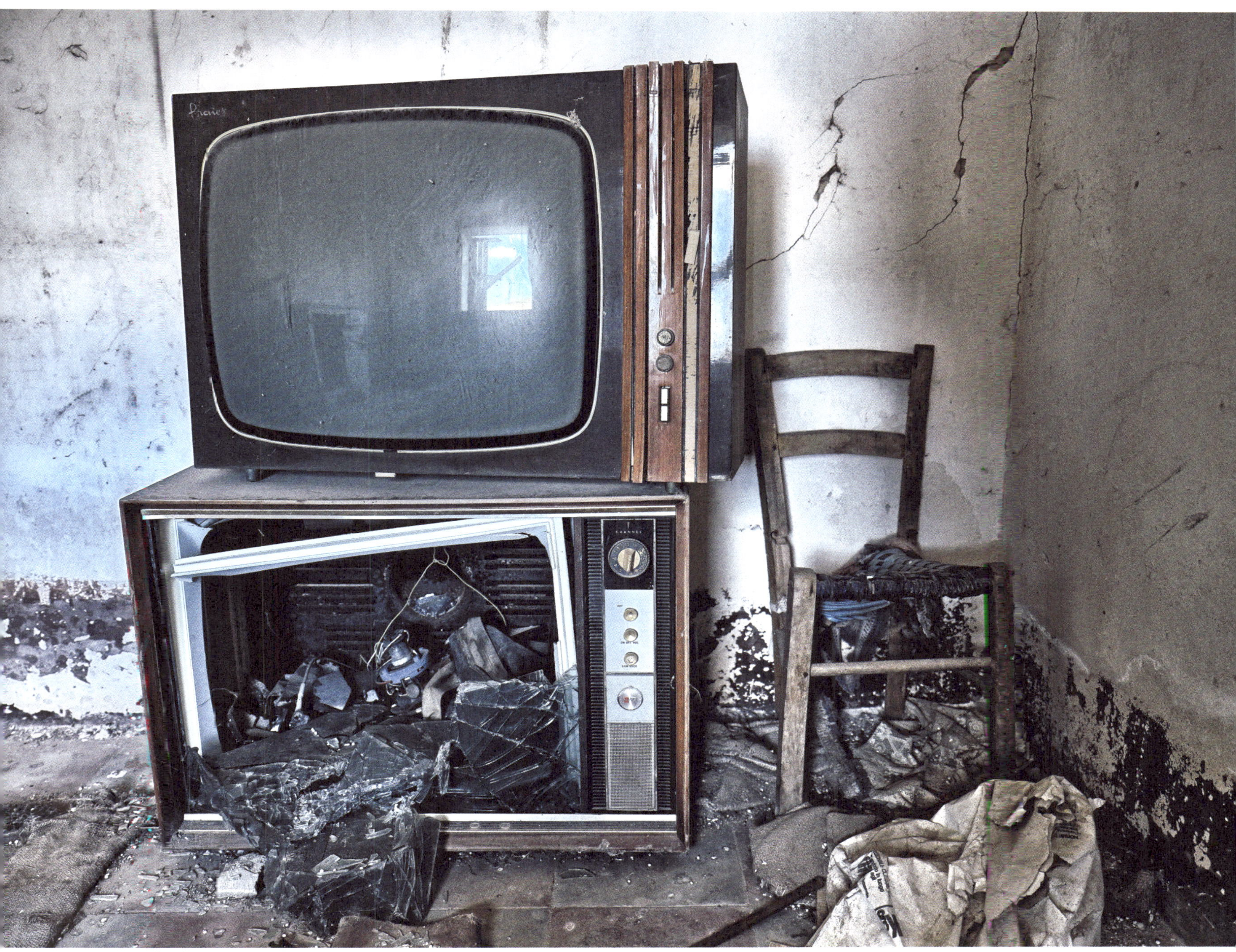

Figure 5

MYLES MCCALLUM

Images of Reform

I have spent many years working in southern Italy as an archaeologist, excavating ancient sites and engaging in archaeological field survey in the vicinity of the buildings photographed by Steven Seidenberg, which are an inescapable element of the local topography. I have a history with these structures, having walked around them and sought shelter within them during inclement weather, a tourist of sorts participating in one of the less common itineraries within the Italian peninsula.

Seidenberg's photographs, which document a mingling of local historical eddies with more powerful international historical currents, evoke powerful feelings of loss and failure. They record the failure to take root, the failure of a system that privileges macroeconomic gains at the expense of individual desires for material comfort and security, a failure in the search for agency in the face of and independence from traditional forces of social, economic, and psychological oppression. The dreams of home and community promised and then denied are captured powerfully and beautifully alongside a sense of futility and failure in the face of powerful external economic forces that privilege lire and the fiscal bottom line over human needs and desires.

Keeping in mind the historical context and turning to the photos themselves, an element of particular interest is how Seidenberg frames them, what he has chosen to focus on and what he has left out of his shots. Within the houses, his shots of the detritus left behind by former occupants and residents are particularly interesting. Rather than framing an object or collection of objects against the backdrop of the entire room in which it now resides, he often focuses on these items to the exclusion of their surroundings. The colors and textures are vivid, as is the sense of decay for those organic materials such as wooden furniture, mattresses, and clothing, and the images are taken from a range of interesting and unusual angles, different from how one passing through the space might view them. At the same time, Seidenberg has eschewed imbuing these structures and their contents with a sense of nostalgia. In this vein, I am drawn to his photo of the two broken television sets, stacked one upon the other, and next to them a badly damaged wooden chair (Figure 5). The room in which these items appear was full of other children's items including a bassinet and broken toys, as well as old clothing, as if it had been curated as a museum of ruination. A different photographer might have tugged at the viewer's heartstrings by focusing on these other items, potentially invoking a maudlin, romantic view of the human past with which these objects are connected. Instead, Seidenberg presents us with a jumbled and puzzling image, with similar and dissimilar objects incongruously arranged, as the houses themselves seem incongruous yet essentially also a part of the layered and textured landscape in which they reside. They witness a failed attempt at continuity, one broken television replaced by another, the new one resting on the old one, objects that instead demonstrate the temporary nature of residence in the house.

In the object photos, the sparseness of the spaces stands out: the lack of furniture—left behind, removed by the original owners, or taken later by scavengers—and the simplicity of what remains—wires stretched across walls and ceilings and nails used as hooks to suspend objects, tools, and photographs. There is a sense of poverty that the photos capture objectively, matter-of-factly, without presenting this poverty as particularly noble. These buildings and the land surrounding them, which were to be a vehicle for the poor to improve their material lot in life, represent material continuity with an impoverished past, continuity of traditional material patterns of consumption. Yet, ultimately, they are a break with the traditional communities of support or meaning in which these impoverished residents were once embedded. The traditional elements contrast starkly with the futuristic or contemporary architecture described below, another element of incongruity. Looking at these images, one wonders what went wrong, how these planned communities could have failed so completely.

There is also a visible connection between the buildings and the landscape, perhaps strengthened by the barrenness and brownness of the summer fields surrounding them. The environment is highly eroded and erodible. The crumbling plateaux, with waves of colluvium descending their sides, and the decaying roads slowly crumbling and disappearing, as if built on a sandy beach and subject to the vagaries of surf and tides, indicate a landscape in a constant state of flux or transformation. There is an inevitable sense that the landscape and all the angular, concrete and stone structures populating it are weathering down to the particles, the brown clay and sand, slowly merging with their surroundings. The use of color in the photos heightens this effect, with the exteriors bleached grey and white—their original colors of red, blue, and pink, faded to the point of erasure—contrast strongly with the brilliant, overpowering yellow and brown of the wheat fields during harvest, which reflects the sunlight blindingly like the surface of an inland ocean. The houses are framed within their backdrop as anomalous blips on the landscape, but, through the process of decay, are now merging with it.

Even as the houses weather into their surroundings they are otherworldly, alien. There is something remarkably incompatible between the futurist architecture of the homes, particularly the single-story houses with the dovecotes and sloping, oddly angled roof-lines covering their stalls and porches (Figure 1). Others take their architectural cues from mid-century suburbia, partaking in a new globalist and consumerist approach to building design. The repetition of nearly identical forms across the plateaux and fields reveals the forces behind their creation (Figure 7). The houses stand out from the cereal monoculture around them and so are clearly visible from great distances throughout the landscape, a highly legible testimony to the failure of the *Riforma* program for the thousands of colonists who once occupied them. The landscape, transformed now into market-oriented agriculture, seems as hospitable to human residence as the surface of the moon.

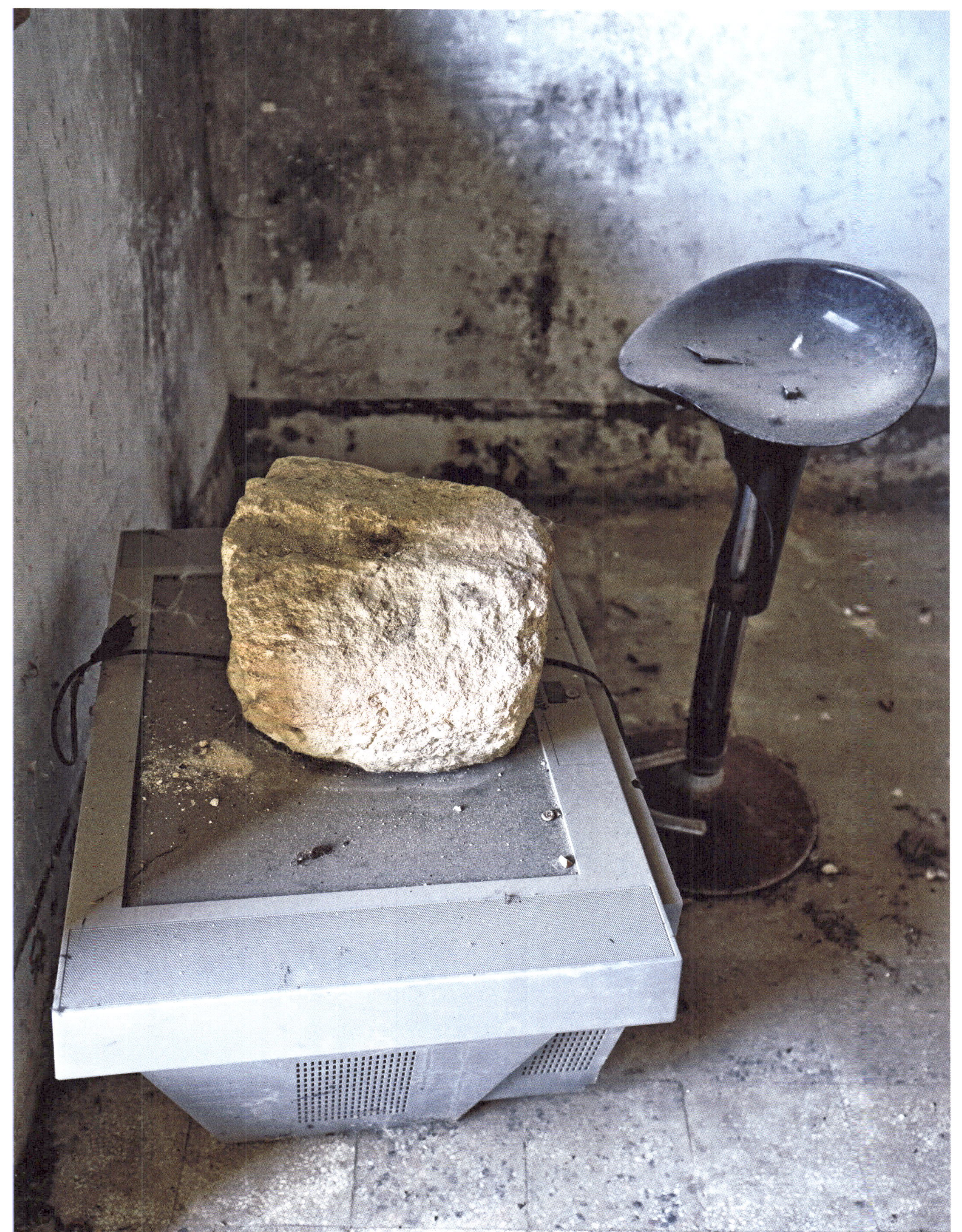

Figure 6

CARMEN BELMONTE

Depicting Abandonment: The *Riforma Fondiaria* as Heritage in Contemporary Italy

An Iconic Image

There is a rural house in a wasteland. The ears of wheat in the foreground rise up and surround the building creating an imaginary barrier to this private space. The *starburst* effect of diffracted sun overshadows the facade and fragments a surface of solids and voids—the porch with its arch, the wall of stone blocks, and the gutted windows. It is just a common rural house but its representation, with a low vantage point and the natural enclosure of the wheat caught in its gentle movement, returns a monumental image[1]. The spontaneous grass that grows around the walls as well as on the roof tiles denounces the abandonment of this house. Nature is reappropriating the materiality and the space of the building, generating a kind of "third landscape."[2] On the upper part of the wall on the discolored and peeled plaster, the inscription "Riforma fondiaria" emerges. As a *peritesto* of the building the inscription explicitly labels and positions it as part of a wider political, economic, and social project.[3] Despite the monumental appearance constructed by the photographic image, the rural architecture—with its state of abandonment revealed in the many details—announces the outcome of the project and sanctions its failure (Figure 10). I use this image as a point of departure to introduce the photographic project *The Architecture of Silence: Abandoned Lives of the Italian South* and to investigate the gaze of Steven Seidenberg, exploring the material legacies of the postwar project of *La Riforma Fondiaria* in the surroundings of Irsina (MT).

In Basilicata, as well as in many other rural areas of the Italian peninsula—from North to South—other similar settlements were erected as part of the ambitious project of agrarian reform promoted by

---

1   Carolyn L. White, Steven Seidenberg, and Myles McCallum, "Disaster for the People, Bonanza for the State. The Riforma Fondiaria in Postwar Italy," *Places Journal* (2019), 5.
2   Gilles Clément, *Manifeste du Tiers-paysage* (Paris, éd. Sujet Objet, 2004); Nadia Breda and Franco Lai, eds., *Antropologia del Terzo paesaggio*, (Rome: CISU, 2011).
3   On the concept of peritext see Gérard Genette, *Seuils* (Paris: Éditions du Seuil, 1987; translated as *Paratexts. Thresholds of interpretation* [Cambridge: CUP, 1997]) and Luca Acquarelli, Michele Cogo, Francesca Tancini, eds., *Il peritesto visivo: copertine e altre strategie di presentazione* (EIC Serie Speciale, Nuova Cultura, 2013).

the government and implemented according to the laws passed in 1950.[4] The project intended to break apart the huge estates owned by wealthy landowners and to distribute the lands to peasants, interested in working on them and modernizing agriculture.[5] The project was supported, for different reasons, by left-wing forces as well as by the *Democrazia Cristiana* (Christian democracy), both of which were interested in promoting the growth of small rural properties. Despite being one of the most prominent state interventions in Italian history, the land reform soon failed. The reasons were various: in many cases the rich owners gave up marginal land of poor quality and obtained huge rewards, which they reinvested in urban centers, contributing to the boom in construction of the following decade. In addition, the average size of the plots of land was often unsuitable to support a whole family and irrigation was insufficient. By the 1960s, a large number of families had left their homes and land organized both in centralized villages and scattered houses, which in some cases were never inhabited.[6] Some of the land today is managed by corporations cultivating wheat, farro, and other grains, but the houses have been used as storages or shelters only sporadically and remain in a state of abandonment.[7]

Exploring Space and Time

> *Space is a doubt: I have constantly to mark it, to designate it. It is never mine, never given to me, I have to conquer it.*[8]

Georges Perec's words capture Seidenberg's conquering of this space, by exploring, crossing, observing, seeing with his camera overviews and details of modern archaeological remains. He leads the viewer through the Lucanian landscape, transformed by the *Ri-*

4   'Legge Stralcio' 841/1950 issued by the government of Alcide De Gasperi; l. 230 /1950 concerning the territory of Regione Calabria and l.r. 104/1950 issued by the Regione Sicilia.
5   Fausto Carmelo Nigrelli, "I paesaggi della riforma agraria. Dalla storia al progetto', in *Quaderni 13, I paesaggi della Riforma Agraria. Storia, pianificazione, gestione*, eds. Fausto Carmelo Nigrelli and Gabriella Bonini (edizioni Istituto Alcide Cervi, 2017), 9.
6   Nigrelli, 10-11.
7   White, Seidenberg, and McCallum, 3.
8   Georges Perec, *Species of Spaces and Other Pieces*, (Penguin, 1974), 91.

forma Fondiaria project, exploring interior and exterior spaces. From the cultivated field of the hilly landscape marked by the rural buildings to single everyday objects present in the houses, the camera catches and highlights the contrast between the defined edges of pastel-colored fields, and the chaotic position of things in the interiors of farmhouses, where liminal spaces are subverted by gutted doors and rubble that obstruct the passage from one room to another.

Tracing a path through the places of land reform, Seidenberg's eye crosses several decades of Italian history and explores lines of continuity and discontinuity spanning from fascism and its agrarian policy to post-war reform, and to the legacies of both in contemporary Italy. It is a journey that starts from space and drops into time. The objects caught in the homes tell of a distant daily life, populated by slippers and toothbrushes, televisions, armchairs and strollers, their brands and peculiar shapes refer to the particular time to which they belong. Seidenberg adopts distinct visual strategies in representing these places. The bewildering still life composed of a stool and an upside-down TV weighted down by a boulder is represented by a fast, almost instinctive shot, as a reportage photography (Figure 6). On the other hand, in front of the room with blue walls, used as a dormitory, he stops and finds a rigorous framing adopting a different visual language, more interested in the documentation of the space and closer to architectural photography (Figure 8).[9] As in an archaeological excavation, he identifies and documents the objects present in the room in their stratification: the rectangular floor tiles, the accumulated soil and dust, a long branch of grass, a bucket. And then the mats, the cartoons, the mattresses, under which a bottle and a glass emerge. Like vertical vectors, the cloths stretched on a wire and a towel hanging on the walls are grafted onto the horizontality of the floor. The original bright color of the paint leaves room for fading and white gaps that allow a glimpse of the underlying layer of plaster, but on the right side of the wall, framed by the wire from which the cloths are hung, overlies a graffito in Arabic. It is a

9   Roberta Valtorta, *Il pensiero dei fotografi. Un percorso nella storia della fotografia dalle origini a oggi*, (Milano: Bruno Mondadori, 2008).

trace of a recent presence. These are the silent lives of migrants, mostly from Africa, involved in picking fruit and vegetables and victims of the *Caporalato*, a new social plague that intersects with the phenomenon of immigration as part with the Mediterranean crisis.[10] More than once, in the depiction of the places of land reform, Seidenberg strategically renounces the representation of the internal environment by choosing frames that force the observer to look beyond the walls—outside the windows, outside the doors—leading him to a liminal space and inviting him to observe the dialogue between inside and outside, contrasting chaos and abandonment with the farmed natural landscape.

The *Riforma Fondiaria* as Cultural Heritage

Recently, regions and municipalities have promoted preservation policies for the rural villages and agrarian landscapes of la *Riforma Fondiaria*, but a unique national strategy has not come together. In particular, the Basilicata Region within the project *Pays. Med. Urban* has elaborated an atlas of the urban landscape which—through photographic documentation—allows an analysis of the landscape of the reform and its evolution of the last decades.[11] The material legacies of *La Riforma* today start to be recognized as heritage at risk and the promotion of combined preservation plans that consider architectural, natural, and agricultural values is part of academic and cultural heritage institutions agendas.[12]

The villages and settlements of the *Riforma Fondiaria* were planned according to a uniform design and to a peculiar typology of construction. The reform dismembered the latifundia and heavily modified the landscape, which in recent decades is changing due to technological innovation in agriculture and to the replacement of

10 Francesco Di Bartolo, "Dalla riforma agraria al capolarato del XXI sec.," in *Quaderni 13, I paesaggi della Riforma Agraria. Storia, pianificazione, gestione*, eds. Fausto Carmelo Nigrelli and Gabriella Bonini (edizioni Istituto Alcide Cervi, 2017), 129-138.
11 Anna Abate and Rosanna Argento, "Le trasformazioni urbane nei luoghi della riforma agraria," *Ri-Vista, ricerche per la progettazione del paesaggio*, luglio-dicembre (2012), 119.
12 Abate and Argento, 120.

poly-cultural techniques in favor of intensive monocultural ones.[13] Therefore, the restoration and protection of these settlements should rebuild the link between the scattered houses or settlements and the surrounding countryside. This would encourage the recovery of agricultural products and traditional land processing techniques, promoting initiatives such as rural social housing or eco-villages. Concerning the urban and architectural plans, the design of the settlements of the *Riforma*, analogous to the villages realized during the fascist Ventennio, adopted traditional technologies of rural architecture, using local stone for masonry and rejecting reinforced concrete since 1940s, because of the autarchy. As landmarks of the local landscape and because they are able to document historical building technologies and materials, the relics of the *Riforma Fondiaria* can be considered "monuments" of the history of the countryside in the first Italian Republic.[14]

However, according to Robert Musil, even the most celebrated monuments at a certain point become immune to public attention and face invisibility.[15] Seidenberg has reactivated their presence through the photographic medium, reinterpreting this material heritage as a critical image of a political project's failure and of abandonment of places in Southern Italy.[16] Indeed, his work is not a systematic documentation of landscape and architectural objects, but it proposes an image of abandonment, a visual representation of the invisible absence. Seidenberg has purged human representation from his shots, but, digging into the interiors, he has accurately recorded the traces of the many lives that temporarily inhabited the houses of

13 Vincenzo Sapienza, "Il progetto della città rurale dall'ECLS all'ERAS. Funzione, forma, materiali e tecniche," in *Quaderni 13, I paesaggi della Riforma Agraria. Storia, pianificazione, gestione*, eds. Fausto Carmelo Nigrelli and Gabriella Bonini (edizioni Istituto Alcide Cervi, 2017), 223-236.
14 Nigrelli, 18.
15 Robert Musil, "Monuments," in *Selected Writings: Young Torless, Three Women, The Perfecting of a Love, and other writings*, ed. Burton Pike (New York: Continuum, 1986), 320-323.
16 The *Abbandonologia* investigates the phenomenon of abandonment in the South of Italy, see Vito Teti, *Quel che resta. L'Italia dei paesi tra abbandoni e ritorni* (Roma: Donzelli, 2017).

traces of the many lives that temporarily inhabited the houses of the *Riforma*, legitimately or illegally, in order to denounce their silent absence. Absent, but at the same time evoked, are those who were the original inhabitants of those houses—the farmers told by Rocco Scotellaro in *Contadini del Sud* [17]—as well as those who later found temporary refuge in those houses, or today's migrant farmworkers from Africa, victims of the *Capolarato*.

By plumbing the multiple layers of the stratified memory of these buildings, Seidenberg assigns to their material current presence the task of *monere*—to remind—the history of a failed reform together with stories of emigration and immigration, of lives on the margins, of disappointed hopes: the abandoned lives of the Italian South.

17 *Contadini del Sud* was published for the first time in 1954 and collects the materials of a survey on the peasant culture in southern Italy, commissioned by the publisher Laterza from Rocco Scotellaro, poet and political activist from Basilicata. It was published again in 1964 together with *L'uva puttanella* in a unique volume with a preface by Carlo Levi.

From the Land Area

And the concrete (ghost) of existence, from the moment in which it had come to yield, could absorb itself in the most undecidable, and so clear, degree of matter. Mummy; crystal. Sparkling, white light. Dead point of, not memory; which staggers, leaving the crumbling of the surfaces the residual compactness the glare of lime. What had already been offered as a use, invisible weaving of the prescribed gestures or more threadlike geometry of habitual movement, from the rotating screech of the alien planet fell like a skin on the gravitational magnet, to cover its entire extent, halting its right degradation for the time of one click, for the beating of a false movement vibrated on the jambs from the heart of the stasis: fixed, it lay on the wall of the moment, on the crack of the shadow that now scratched it from the afterlife, as in the cutting line the slow razor of light.

From the noise around, of the parched fields, from a desert of crops, the echo of the ancient revolts, the occupation of the unfruitful lands, the conquests of the field fights, the law excerpt, then, the land re-distribution, the disregard of the years, the seed bitter of the earth, the departure of the children towards an industrial dream, everything was printed in a row on the peeling screen of those walls, as in the decal, from the time of the last abandonment, of the departure for different and more distant planets; and it floated invisible from the wind penetrated by the fixtures, jelly spread over the attics, on the ossified inventory of objects, projected its spectrum of inanimate lights like a film, traced the already extinct course of generations. Only an icon, like an anchorite carved on the creaking of a door, was now printed on the threshold of silence, their guardian demon; and the tumult of the many opalescences, crowding from the back of the room, pressed to break the occlusion of the diaphragm, which held them back, in the shadow spread beyond the veil of the, ever more, visible, of the sucked away into the depths of the spaces.

The rotation of the lenses, the probe squeezing, widening, from the dead center of this area that had exploded, disintegrating its alien turn of screw, was burying the fossils of a more remote act, absorbed in the depths of its nuclear time, was sinking like a blade into the extraneous stillness of that Mediterranean light, now so unnatural. Thus the optical excavation was opening tunnels in the stratigraphies of what had been set aside, was exploring its fabrics, fibers, veins, furnishings, the shadow which remained impressed, as in the radio flash of a shroud, the focal crystal of a new disincarnation. And it was then unfolding, from the glass membrane, like an entire archaeology of past lives, in their fragments their grist essences: which, drawn away for a short turn of decades, sucked back like in a milky channel, through the magnet of a ray, migrated to other worlds from the narrow time of two or three generations, was collapsing now on its point of no return, was emitting its extreme, exhausted gleam in discontinuous waves, was radiating, in short beams, its last carnival of ghosts.

Thus we were exploring, one by one, the finds pushed up by that shine, following the short hum of the shots without distinguishing their origin; printed on the peeling of the plaster, the arcane trace of a detonation that never happened, already sucked into the bolus of history, was pouring, as in negative, as invisible mold, the re-emerged appearance of a world, the distant murmur of a never-ending passage. And if a conjecture of existence was persisting, it did not leak from the bulk of the residual materials, the mineral regression of the objects, or from the unmade walls of its ancient delimitation and living, but from that alien imprint released on the door that continued here to sun itself, demon or fetish, the guardian of shadows put there to suppress any, impossibility of, memory.

And always the day was clear here like crystal, sharpened by the razor of light. From picture to picture, surrounding the smallness of the rooms the fossil sound of what was deserted the opaque wreck, so, of such an intense glow, the optical probe was redirecting, in spurts, the sense of its movement: thus, the frames transmitted to us were going to compose themselves in the silent continuity of a sequence, which no wall would have been able to delimit anymore. And re-emerging, the deserted eye of the probe, from the opalescent background of every disappearance that had always happened here, was overturning its Albertian point of vision, was moving within the dense network of cracks of that interrupted time, out of phase since always, was creeping into the silent gasp of the infinite degradation of the materials and in the continuation of their imperceptible murmur, as if ascending a depth of constellations, in the temporality of that after-bomb solarization.

So following the single footprint of the hum, an already forgotten idea of nature, of fibrillated lifeless nature, was suddenly found afloat: almost ectoplasm from the putrefaction of the objects, it was projecting from the fading of the frames, to push us upwards through the vent of a sudden extinction. As if to be born, to be born to be born again to disappear again, as if to give birth to us again, by climbing the tail of its light-year flash. And then we would have drunk the milk of the light, sucking by the crystal probe as if its eye were a nipple for us: that it could pour out, in jerks, here up to us, up to the desert that in the marrow drains us to infinity, here it could pour out its dazzling vanishing: so that our exhausted fibers could feed, up to the thinnest nerve, of that soul flesh, up to the thinnest nerve: the flesh from which we had to take leave, inside the sharp day of the crystal, and slip away into the deafening roar of the countrysice.

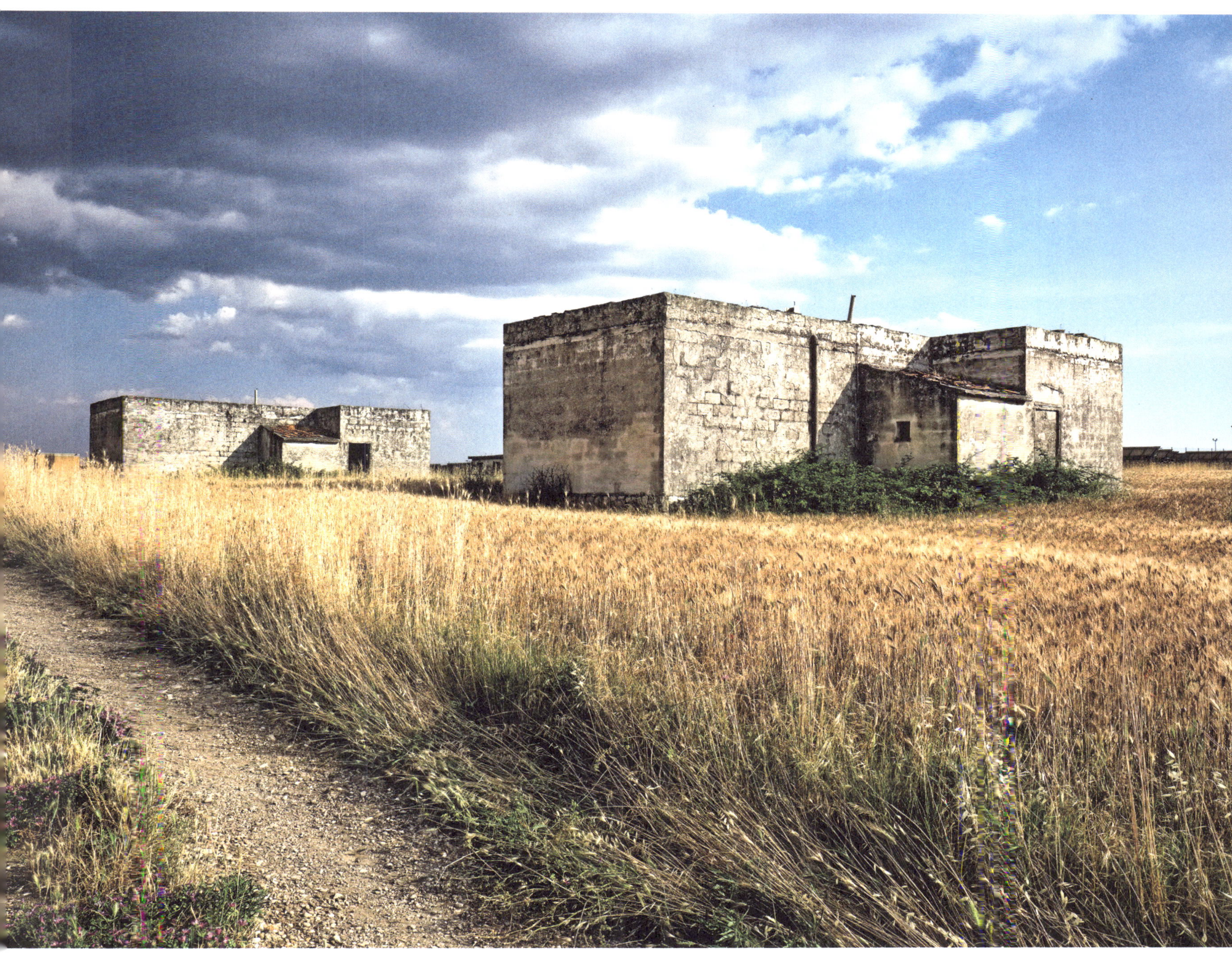

Figure 7

JILKE GOLBACH

Ruination by Reform:
"Don't Let the Big Men Take It Away from You"

One of the most unsettling things in Steven Seidenberg's photographs of the abandoned homes of the *Riforma Fondiaria* is the impression of their complete and utter disconnection. In the yellow-green fields of the Italian south, the small settlements appear cut off from any form of human life as if sprung up from the same soil as the weeds that surround them. No roads or paths connect the homes to nearby towns or villages, no terraces or fences create margins between inside and out, and no hint of departures or arrivals clings to doorsteps that disappear into nowhere. Even the land is worked and ploughed right up to their walls, the evidence of machines still visible in curved lines that follow the slopes and dips of the landscape by which the homes are gradually being reclaimed (Figure 11).

The effect is an alienating, disorienting view of erasure and abandonment that is haunting yet strangely familiar. Other images of deserted homes come to mind, in particular the documents produced by Farm Security Administration (FSA) photographers during the disastrous Depression years of 1930s America when a breakdown of traditional modes of agricultural production in conjunction with economic and environmental crises led to one of the largest waves of human migration in the history of the West.

Some of those images show that then, too, tractors ran right up to the houses—no matter if they had been long deserted or barely vacated. Entire families were evicted and substituted with a single machine, pushed out by tractors that performed gestures of cold-blooded destruction, wiping out human presence by churning over dusty earth. "Across the dooryard the tractor cut, and the hard, foot-beaten ground was seeded field, and the tractor cut through again; the uncut space was ten feet wide. And back he came," wrote John Steinbeck in *The Grapes of Wrath* of such an instance of erasure. "The iron guard bit into the house-corner, crumbled the wall, and wretched the little house from its foundation so that it fell sideways, crushed like a bug."

Although seemingly worlds apart, the abandoned farm houses of Depression-era America and those of the *Riforma Fondiaria* in postwar Italy are connected not only by such potent visual tropes but by the very systems of reform that produced this kind of rural decay in the first place. The systems crushed not just homes but entire livelihoods like bugs in the process. Both the economic crisis of the 1930s and the Second World War gave rise to redistributionist agendas that were constructed on comparable ideologies of agricultural reform rooted in the American presidency of Franklin D. Roosevelt, first as part of the New Deal and later repurposed in the Marshall Plan. Both agendas were designed to benefit those at the very bottom of society, yet often ended up working disproportionately to the advantage of big business.

The ill-conceived *Riforma Fondiaria* program, concocted by the Italian government and its American allies under the umbrella of the Marshall Plan, might have been an effort to redistribute wealth from large landowners to dispossessed peasants, but its ideological foundations were more than a little shaky. Based on a romantic vision of land ownership and family farming, which had already proven outdated and ineffective during the New Deal years in the U.S., the program was propped up by the appropriation of socialist strategies that were superficially applied but not carried through. The result was an epic failure of a program, the material consequences of which are captured in this book. Most *Riforma* tenants were forced out in under two years by the sheer impossibility of making the poor land work for them. And those that reaped the benefits were the state, who resold the land at profit, and large agricultural corporations, who now possess and exploit it.

In 1938, FSA photographer Dorothea Lange captured a slogan along a highway in California that read, "This is your country, don't let the big men take it away from you." At a time when scores of small family farms and tenant farmers were going under because of the mechanization and industrialization of agriculture the meaning of this message would have been instantly clear. Not only were banks and corporations reclaiming large swathes of land to make profitable with modern machines rather than manual labour, farmers also faced a sharp drop in prices as a result of the sudden over-production of goods. Combined, these factors formed the main cause for rural abandonment in the Depression years as many farming families were driven out of their homes and off their land, even when the droughts and dust storms that tormented the Dust Bowl states in the mid-1930s are taken into consideration.

In response to the catastrophic consequences of the Great Depression, Roosevelt's New Deal sought to redistribute income, relieve poverty, and reform the U.S. economy. In some respects its programs offered (quite literally) a lifeline to the many victims of the Depression and produced long-lasting legacies that formed the foundation for a modern welfare state—accomplishments achieved not least because of the efforts of the FSA photographers to bring the unprecedented scale of suffering around the country into sharp focus. But in the field of agriculture the New Deal's strategies and incentives were all wrong. In an attempt to correct the falling farm prices, the government offered subsidies to landlords and large-scale agribusiness to reduce their production. Instead of aid trickling down to tenant farmers and sharecroppers, however, the money was used to purchase more machines and further reduce the need for manual labour, producing quite the opposite effect.

Another consequence of agricultural industrialization in the 1930s was that it produced the need for seasonal rather than year-round labour as most activities previously done by hand were mechanized. This created a vicious system in which tens if not hundreds of thousands of migrant workers were hopelessly caught during the harshest years of the Depression, including those tenant farmers who had been evicted elsewhere. Often, their only chance of survival was to follow the crop harvest from field to field, county to county, all the while filling the pockets of grand landowners. In modern Italy, the abandoned houses of the *Riforma* testify to a different kind of migrant figure. Signs of transient existence among the homes' material remains speak of the precarious lives of displaced people and economic migrants who occasionally seek shelter in these outbuildings, some of them escaping countries whose severe economic inequalities and high poverty levels are in themselves a by-product of the profit-seeking mechanisms on which our global capitalist system is built.

It has often been said that the Second World War, not the New Deal, brought an end to the Depression. The much mythologised Marshall Plan that was implemented in its wake exported New Deal tactics and funnelled aid into Europe as part of a concealed effort to consolidate capitalism and counter the influence of communism on the continent. The recovery program was intended to help rebuild the economies of European nations but once again benefited large corporations in a disproportionate way. The failure of the *Riforma Fondiaria* scheme in Italy in particular had many causes, not least the failure of the state to deliver the promised infrastructures and the deprived conditions of the recipients' semi-isolated existence. But the marginality of the land that was redistributed, both with regards to size and quality, was a major factor. The nostalgic idea of giving back small plots of land to landless peasants as a means to achieve self-sustenance and economic independence was not only a gross misunderstanding of the changed realities of the agricultural business in the post-war era but also a complete ignorance of lessons learned from the New Deal.

Seidenberg's photography of the ruins of the *Riforma* employs a visual language that foregrounds matter and form in its exploration of deserted homes as symbols of the "broken promises of post-war neoliberalism," as Carolyn L. White describes in her introduction. In recent years, much has been written on the photography of ruins and the contemporary obsession with images of decay. The category of 'ruin porn' is now standard terminology for representations of ruins that are considered to be of aesthetic appeal but are deemed to fetishize, romanticize, or trivialize the social realities at the centre of dereliction. The validity of such criticisms needs to be carefully scrutinised, however, since these comments are often rooted in superficial understandings of what photographic images have the power (or not) to do while undervaluing the critical potential of material approaches.

Although images of dereliction are now common, the Farm Security Administration photographs are widely considered to be the first documentary images of rural decay. As such, they can be understood as a point of departure for the long lineage of ruin photography that followed. The project's original focus was oriented specifically, although not exclusively, toward the social and economic relations of American agricultural labor, and the purpose was to garner public support for New Deal policies. Its humanitarian premise is still widely celebrated today and most of the by-now iconic images are portraits of people. But the FSA photographers also produced a suite of images that were devoid of people, acutely aware that at times the material or the non-human produces the greatest emotional or political affect.

Seidenberg's photographs harness this power to combine the critical with the material-aesthetic in compositions that flatten the shapes, forms, and textures of abandoned possessions and broken interiors to the point of abstraction. As David Campany once said about FSA photographer Walker Evans, he "was not exactly making abstract art out of photography but using photography to point to abstraction as it occurs out in the world." The same might be said of Seidenberg whose way of seeing critiques the conditions of marginal human lives and the systems that produce them through carefully composed pictures of the material worlds that are left behind.

The historical and visual patterns that emerged between the crises of 1930s America and post-war Italy help to interpret these photographs as records of a neoliberal capitalism that manages to squeeze profit out of even the most marginalised. As Seidenberg's images show, the 'big men' are still at work, and photography remains a powerful tool in the struggle against their domination.

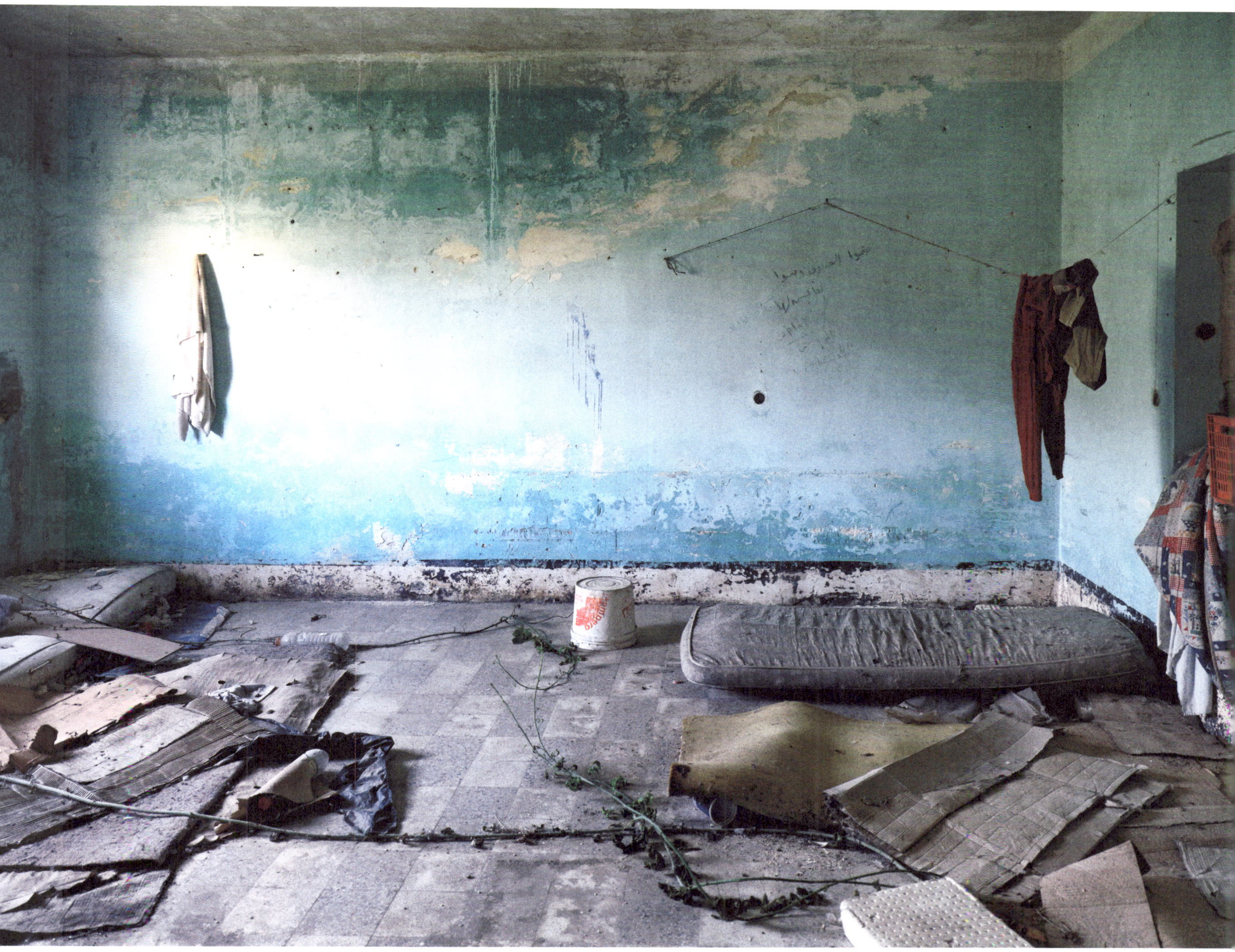

Figure 8

A l Abandoned Houses Look Alike

All abandoned houses look alike. It doesn't matter whether they are large or small, poor or rich, if they are in Europe or America or Asia. All abandoned houses look alike, because they produce similar thoughts in the person who looks at them. (Someone, whom I don't know and almost certainly will never know, walked on this floor, hung a jacket on that hanger, watched his or her favorite show on the TV which has been left in a corner. This someone no longer lives here, but I feel their presence, I cannot ignore it. Indeed, their presence-absence dominates the house).

An Abandoned House Is a Dead Body

All abandoned houses make us think of death. Deprived of the life that once dwelt there, an abandoned house is a body that has stopped being alive. Perhaps this body, the house, may will once again be inhabited, it may be able to be resurrected, but at this moment the abandonment that inhabits the house is stronger than the life that inhabited it. Stronger than the people who used to live here. Stronger than the people who may live here in the future. Stronger than the people who will come to live here.

Photographing Ghosts

Photographing an abandoned house is a difficult exercise. Those who photograph an abandoned house try, whether they are aware of it or not, to photograph what they do not see. Anyone who photographs an abandoned house tries to photograph ghosts. Their gaze, even before their photographic device, tries to trace the signs that locate that house in space and time, which make it unique, different from all the other abandoned houses. A pair of old slippers arranged at an angle on the floor next to a crumpled-up sheet of paper and a worn-out toothbrush. The dusty skeleton of a baby stroller. The carcass of a sofa. Objects that have been used every day for weeks, months, years. Objects that have become skeletons and carcasses. As in an archaeological site of the present time, matter is opposed to abandonment.

Ghosts are Silent, Objects Speak

Before carrying out the *Architecture of Silence: Abandoned Lives of the Italian South* project together with Carolyn L. White, Steven Seidenberg published a book of photographs, *Pipevalve: Berlin* (Lodima Press, 2015). The images frame old pipevalves in an area of the German capital. Short texts follow the photographs. In one of these aphorisms Seidenberg writes: "I stick to one rule: never attack." Not to attack means to remain still, it means to respect. To respect, from the Latin *respicere*, is to look back, to leave a cavity between oneself and the other, to allow a moment of waiting that can also embrace the past. Whether it's the Berlin pipevalves or the abandoned houses of the Italian South, Seidenberg stops, waits. (*Aspectare*, look carefully). Wait for the objects, the walls, the doors and the windows, the space around, to look at him, to welcome his alien presence, to talk to him. And objects speak. There, in Berlin, it was the rusty metal totems that reaffirmed their tenacious resistance to change. Here, between Apulia and Basilicata, things and spaces refer to a daily life reduced to the essentials: an extractor fan blackened by smoke tells of foods cooked and consumed by the fire, the clothes lines that stretch through the rooms continue to curve, as if they were still supporting the weight now vanished from the linen and clothes that once hung there, the mattresses thrown on the ground are old lifeboats for the labors of a day lost in memory.

Abandoned Houses are Black Holes, But It's Sunny Outside

Abandoned houses are black holes. We sink into them, attracted by a gigantic centripetal force. The houses abandoned by their inhabitants try to hold on to those who visit them, to prevent the tragedy of abandonment from happening again. Seidenberg knows this, he does not shy away from this claim. He gives his time and gives himself time. But he doesn't forget that there is an outside, the outside from which he comes, the outside towards which those who occupied these spaces have gone. In fact, he tries to reproduce their gaze when the house was alive. He aims the lens of his camera so that the sun's rays are reflected in the mirror above the lopsided dresser, that the frame of an opening is projected onto the screen of the old bulky television, that the golden pattern of a wheat field penetrates through the square frame of a window. Finally, he goes out. He finds the external space, the external gaze, the sky.

Is Abandonment a Failure?

There was a time when someone—woman, man, child—entered this house for the first time and looked at it, looking into the future. They imagined themselves in this space, arranged their objects. There was a time when someone lived in this house in what was the present for them, moved between things, entered and left without looking around, because habit tarnishes the gaze. There was a moment when someone looked at this house, this space, in the past, imagining themselves in an unknown elsewhere, yet powerful as a magnet. Is it a failure to imagine yourself elsewhere?

An old French popular proverb says: "Tout passe, tout lasse, tout casse et tout se remplace." Is it a failure?

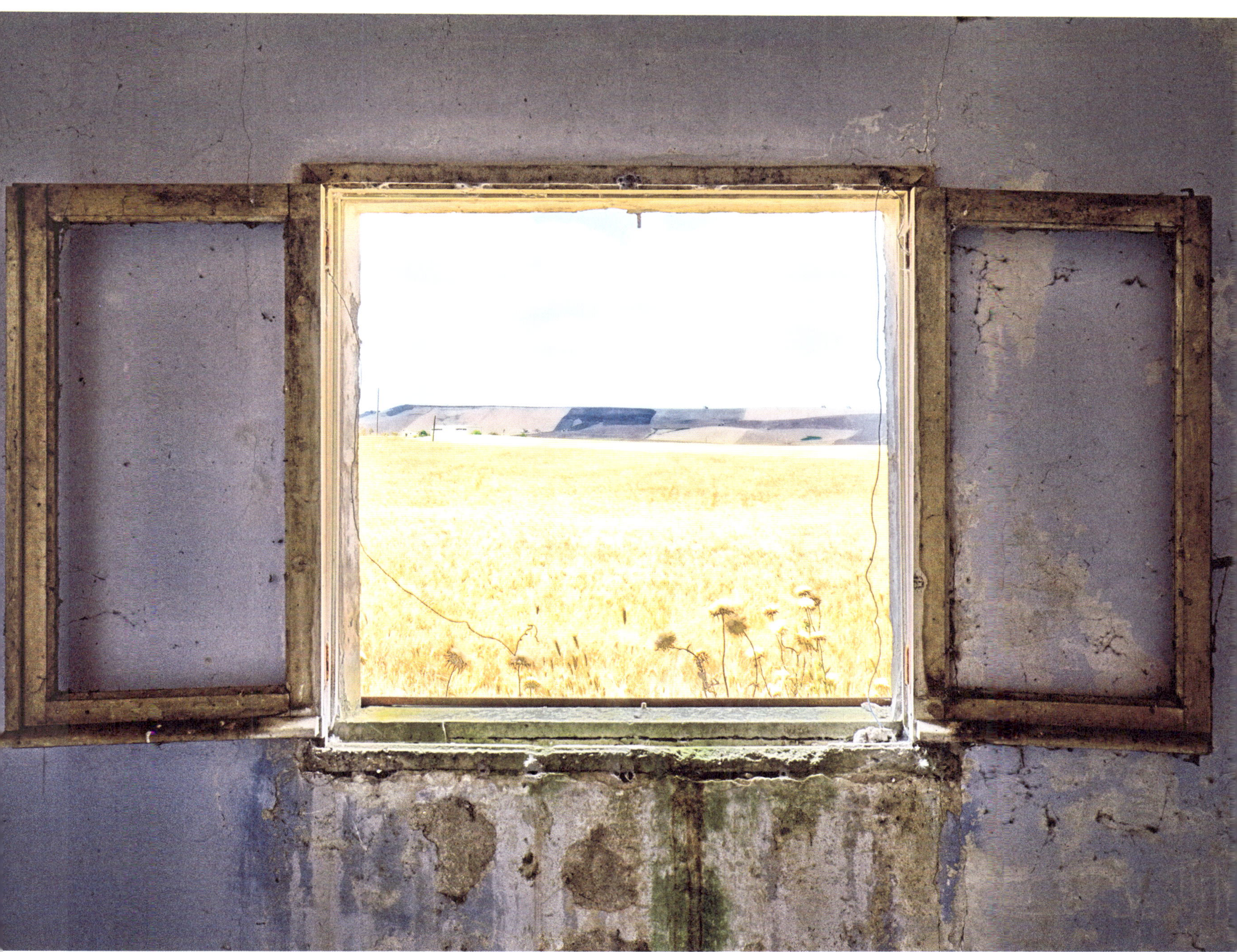

Figure 9

ANTONIO RIELLO

A Reluctant Prophecy

The Southern Italy countryside portrayed by Steven Seidenberg is the blatant and material evidence of a political project deeply rooted in modern Italian History. Maybe more a recurrent dream rather than just a project itself. The "Graal" of the process of Italian unification; the eponymous (and in fact almost legendary) "Questione Meridionale," still in the political agenda of every government since the year 1861.

This is not just the visual debris of a lost ideal, or, from another perspective, the picture of a forgotten and picturesque corner of Italy. These dilapidated houses mean much more—they symbolize ambiguously a sort of unstoppable downgrade affecting the moral compass of the whole Western Civilization (the artistic expression has always a certain subtle degree of vital ambiguity, and Seidenberg's visual research definitely belongs to Art). Considering mostly the last twenty years we can admire, like in a "Historical Peephole," the Time passing by and the resulting decaying of political ambitions and achievements. And as well we are somehow in front of the scattering discomfort of an ominous future, felt currently harder than the recent past. One could actually recognize, in this filthy broken wall or in that dusty relic of furniture, possible anticipations of our common close future. Indeed a clever innuendo about an unhappy and bleak Weltanschauung.

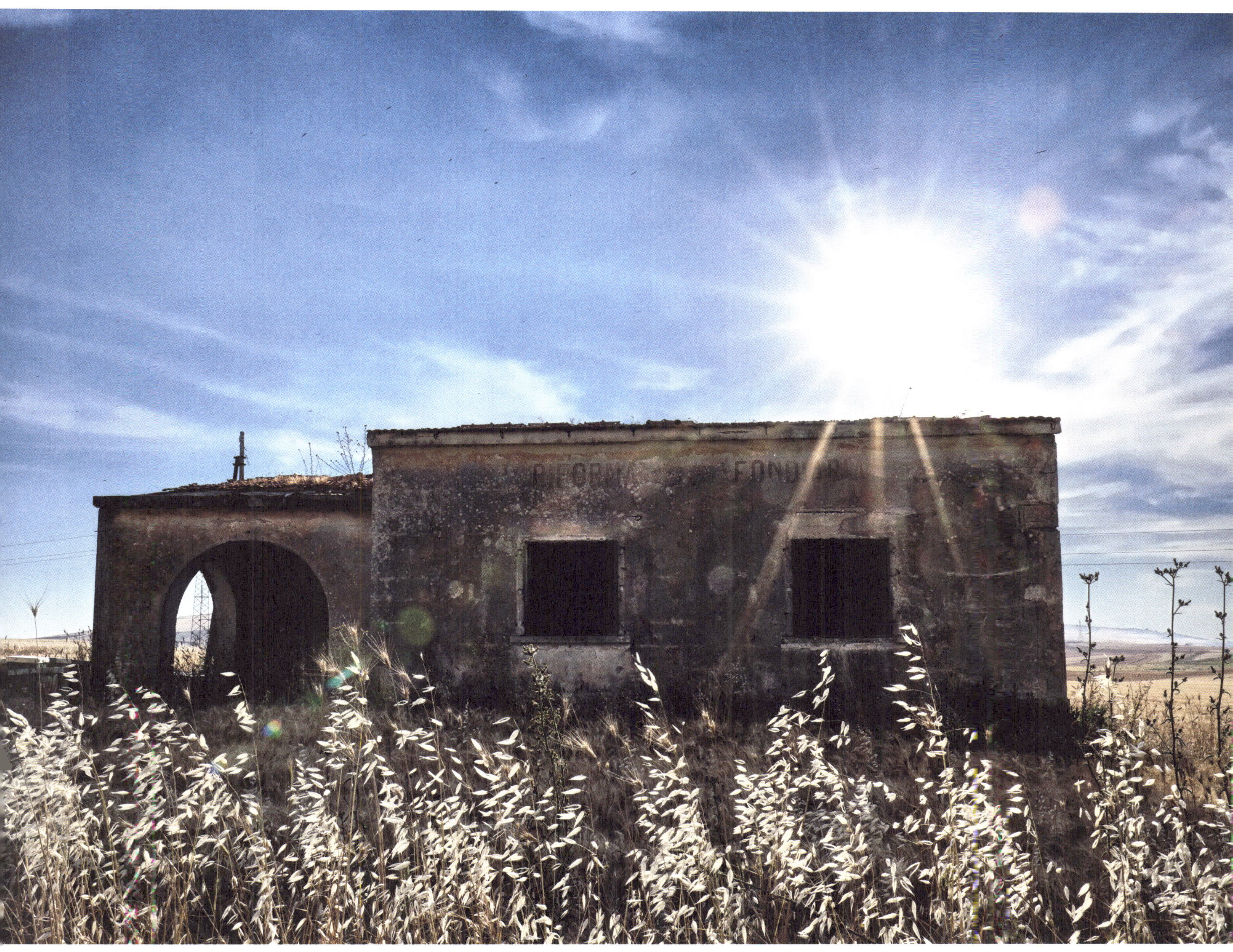

Figure 10

Memory Work

The struggle over the grip of commodification is, in the first instance, a contest between contending visions and values of life and work.[1]

We end on the monument, on the site of memory declaring itself— RIFORMA FONDIARIA—land *re*-formed, *re*-made (Figure 10). The inscription is fading, but this simple statement neatly conveys the continued resonance of a particular historical moment on the land- scape: a brief period with lasting social, economic, and material re- percussions. The remaking of landscapes is a complex process that often involves political force, physical intervention, and aesthetic mediation. Seidenberg's images of the *Riforma Fondiaria* prompt me to think about the role photography has played and continues to play in these interconnected processes, and about the possible re-conceptualization of such sites as heritage. Both of these threads are ultimately about the different ways in which value—social, eco- nomic, historic, aesthetic, therapeutic, or otherwise—is coaxed out of and etched onto the world. To what extent might photography engage with the contested visions of life and work that competing notions of value evoke? A speculative reading of the landscapes and buildings of the agrarian reform *as heritage* allows us to see how this relationship might unfold.

Photographs do not simply produce or construct heritage value, but they do occupy an important place in the broader ecologies through which different values are assigned to and extracted from the world. Most noticeably, the production, circulation, and con- sumption of photographic images routinely supports other technol- ogies of mapping, surveying, documenting, and quantifying a broad array of human and non-human phenomena. This intellectual and symbolic labor may reinforce or contradict the manifold processes through which other forces (geological, biological, chemical, algo- rithmic) work into and on the world. Following Jason Moore's co- ceptualization of capitalism in the web of life, photography's aes- thetic register cannot be divorced from these wider ecologies of

1   Jason W. Moore, "The Capitalocene Part II: accumulation by appropriation and the centrality of unpaid work/energy," *The Journal of Peasant Studies* 45(2), 257.

natural and cultural *work*, which may take many forms and operate to diverse ends.

Why should this matter in the context of the *Riforma Fondiaria* images? A first point to note here is that Seidenberg's photographs document a landscape reworked by capitalism twice over since the end of the Second World War: first with the agrarian reform itself, and then again through the intervention of large scale corporations turning the land over to wheat, farro, and other grains. The latter of these transformations could not have happened without the former; a familiar story of corporate entities capitalizing on state investment and the historical labor of marginalized individuals and communities. While the narrative thrust of the *Riforma Fondiaria* series emerges from and circles back to this sense of failed productivity, subsequent abandonment, and eventual marketization (of the land at least), Seidenberg's images also capture an expanded inventory of work and labor: the weathering effects of wind and rain; the destructive growth of trees and plants; the peculiar human urge to assemble and demolish. What I would like to suggest is that *this* work, commonly gathered under the broad heading of decay, is also highly generative and open to various forms of symbolic recoding.

From Detroit to Varosha, Pripyat to Hashima Island, we are familiar with how this process typically unfolds: striking images of abandonment and ruin document the faded grandeur and haunting atmospheres of post-conflict, post-industrial, or post-disaster sites and landscapes. The prefix is important here because such photographs always register a belated engagement with the event or time they reference, sending the viewer "back to a space behind the image which must forever remain 'off-frame': the distant past."[2]

And—more often than not—this archaeological gaze transforms the site depicted. Sometimes slowly, sometimes with alarming alacrity,

2   Kitty Hauser, *Shadow Sites: Photography, Archaeology, and the British Landscape 1927-1955* (Oxford: Oxford University Press, 2007), 89.

the abandoned spaces of the world are turned into dark or negative heritage, a recoding that opens them up to the twin logics of preservation and commodification.

It would be easy to place Seidenberg's images in this genealogy, but this would ignore some important dimensions of the *Riforma Fondiaria* series. It would also play into an extractivist view of heritage and photography that needs challenging at every turn. Let us speculate then—using Seidenberg's images as a critical point of departure—on what a counter-heritage of the *Riforma Fondiaria* might look like. First, some key tropes of the heritage canon would need to be jettisoned or, at the very least, refined. A static sense of "preservation," for example, seems wholly unsuited to such dynamic contexts. The ongoing movement of matter across and within these supposedly empty environments subverts human-centric registers of space and time. Seidenberg's photographs may document an absence of social life, but they are teeming with presence in another mode, at once spectral and organic. "Interpretation" would also need a fundamental rethink in this framework. What histories and what knowledge can be teased out from cracked walls, unhinged doors, and smashed chairs? Archaeology can offer us a way in here, but such objects present a challenge to the epistemologies typically foregrounded in this discipline. Perhaps we would need to listen instead to the wheat and the farro: grains that—like all plants—have their own way of interpreting the world.

The most crucial counter movement to be made in this context, however, would be that against commodification. Photography and heritage both work to unearth various categories of value from the historic and natural environment, but this does not need to be in the service of profit-making or economic growth. Indeed, Seidenberg's images might direct us toward other modes of reparation and regeneration, other ways of *giving back* for the work and labor that helped create such haunting spaces in the first place. Photography's memorial capacity is also always a space of resistance against fixed renderings of the past. The "heritage" of the *Riforma Fondiaria* still contains this possibility for doing and thinking memory otherwise;

not as a monument to one version of history, but as a complex inheritance at once fragile and despotic.

Can any image or photographic series really provoke this kind of counter-heritage? Certainly not alone. Such a process will always depend on the broader ecologies in which photographs are produced and positioned—on the way images emerge from and move through the world with varying levels of inertia, poise, and friction. This book and these words are part of this ecology, but the work they might yet perform is still uncertain.

Deforming the Reform

What a thing means is not more important than what it is.[1]

A place that has dismissed its function does not fade away. It takes on a life of its own, as if it had branched off from a hidden root. If the place was generated by human hand, that new life will be protected from humans, by inventing a language alien to them. The very lack of human interference will allow its presence to be transmitted from generation to generation, through its movement toward decay and toward a constant re-making of itself. It is a totemic presence that does not allow for interpretation, words, or poetry. It is being tested against all sense.

The houses built by the *Riforma Agraria* in the Fifties of the twentieth century changed the identity of the fields in the Southern Italian regions that they occupied. The fields, until then bearing the burden of the ancient—or archaic—political identity of territory owned by a few landowners, turned their essence and appearance into the political phenomenon of distribution: if they had made sense from the central panopticon perspective of the castle, now they started making sense from a multi-perspectival view. Farmers were invited to make the change, to make the houses, to inhabit them, to become owners, to become other than what they used to be. The 'face' of the soil put on the mask of democracy and imagination of ransom and promise. Trodding its ground was more than walking. Building a house was more than working as carpenters. The political investment entered the bodies, turning them into agents of enterprise, an idea alien to Italian history, which have delivered over the centuries a culture of fatalism, a constant sensation of being acted upon by stronger and incomprehensible political and natural forces, with the consequent development of a subtle *astuzia*: the ability of getting around the problems, finding stratagems to avoid the feeling of powerlessness, being in a constant state of alarm and mistrust of the others, when they do not belong to family or village.

1   George Kubler, *The Shape of Time: Remarks on the History of Things* (Yale University Press, 1962), 126.

Now they could master the fields, they could do it without coming to terms with anything other than nature. There must have been a new sensation of future time. A new version of the land as source of wealth seemed to replace the modern industrialization and urbanization that had appeared as a mobile source of welfare; for an instant—a historical and unrepeatable instant of time—history invested in the present and reversed it. The land looked like that surface possessed by all and none; it must have appeared as the fulcrum of another challenge: beyond and against the Soviet trust in industry and the past Fascist trust in autarchy, this political chance given to the farmers produced a by-product, a land that passed from owner to owner, satisfying immediate needs, as it must have been in prehistoric times; occupying it meant to be displaced, mobile, dynamic. Back to that primitive impulse, we imagine fatalist farmers welcoming anxiety, enthusiasm, spirit of enterprise, deep change in the secular immobility attributed to them.

And then the crash: the land does not render what it promised; the expenses are not affordable; the house lacks technological apparatuses; the price is too high, the politicians confirm their (archaic?) cynicism. One by one, the families go, migrate to Northern Italy or abroad. They leave behind the traces of that betrayed future.

This series of events, reproduced on fast-forward, speaks about a silence. No one there has a political voice, no one in the rest of the peninsula knows about it and if they do, they take it with the usual fatalism. Some destroy, others are destroyed.

It is at this moment that the traces of the houses break that silence. They are the resilient matter that was planned to be meaningful, and now is molded by what is left out of that meaning. The lacuna that these traces reveal opens up their being that needed destruction of the human in order to come to life; after being objects, tools, functions, and signals of something else (adherent signals, as George Kubler says),[2] they are signals of themselves, self-signals

2   *Ibid*.

that require great effort on the part of the viewers to admit the shock of their presence and to avoid comments, explanations, emotional investment. With these images in their eyes, saying anything is seldom better than saying nothing — as Wittgenstein said about talking of art.

These material entities construct an alphabet devoid of meaning, of any other coordinates than the resonance of their presence. It is not discourse (to be found in historical documents) so much as it is an interpellation of the viewers. History books about the *Riforma* cannot reach into this absolute particular that silently shows itself. It would require a history of things that detects their being, exhibitions of the ways they were used, modified, worn out, recycled, and also of the ways they changed places, people, other objects, the environment.

When confronted with these non-objective things, we cannot treat them as illustrations of historical events; they are too strong to surrender to generalized meanings, or they are too weak to afford any correspondence to purposeful descriptions.

Their being 'past' is here and now; they emerge after the present, if we start from the future that announces their discovery. Their plurality is irreducible: each house, each artifact has left a different trace. Not being images, nor symbols, nor icons, nor ruins, they engage the onlookers in an affective bond. We re-invent their thingness as they re-shape our perceptions. The result is a relationship of intimacy, a liberation from the human agency and the restoration of a non-human environment.

They reveal the thingness of objects, as Heidegger would have it. But even revelation is too human; they rather liberate from the need of revelation, being a mere occurrence. The deformed arrangement of their material parts did not occur all of a sudden; over a non-linear time lapse they started losing their adequacy and their passivity as tools. The relationship the ruins establish between life and death is reversed: the increasing and constant discrepancy of parts made them silent and created that irreversible irreducible particular. The deformed parts created new spaces between them, and new wholes: an inversion of time.

Their being an 'occurrence' appears where, squeezed between what is left of a mattress, or concealed beneath the tilted bricks of a wall, crushed inside the plane of a table, there must be micro-particles of blood cells, skin tissue, the salt of tears, bread crumbs, candle wax, containing some chemistry of hope, hate, suffering, dismal, despair and rebirth: at last invisible monuments to respect.

Totemic layer upon layer, their language is time: a present projected into the past and their being the future story from the past perspective.

Farmers fleeing the place left objects and possessions behind and, once they found new jobs and lives elsewhere, they guaranteed this silent agency. They exert a power on us, though in different ways: as Italian people, we merge with that silent landscape, we have it in our culture, education, and habits and we feel co-responsible for it; it is too familiar for us to notice it and give it the gift of exceptionality. Where were *we*, when that happened? No matter if we weren't born or were kids, we were going to be part and accomplices of what needed publicity to be accomplished—or rather to be left unaccomplished: it needed publicity to replace the real thing. And then it needed silence to hide the failure. It has taken observers from outside—the artist's eye and the anthropologist's eye—to see the trace of time and listen to the things devoid of *us*, to show the agency of things on us; or it has taken a return to Europe, to break that silence and to respect that mute declaration of existence. Through their eyes we come to know that the people who dreamt of living their whole lives here were the unaware *relais* between political strategies and pieces of architecture, doors, windows, tv sets, mattresses, and sofas, that by leaving the houses, the fields took those objects in strange nests, and they hatched.

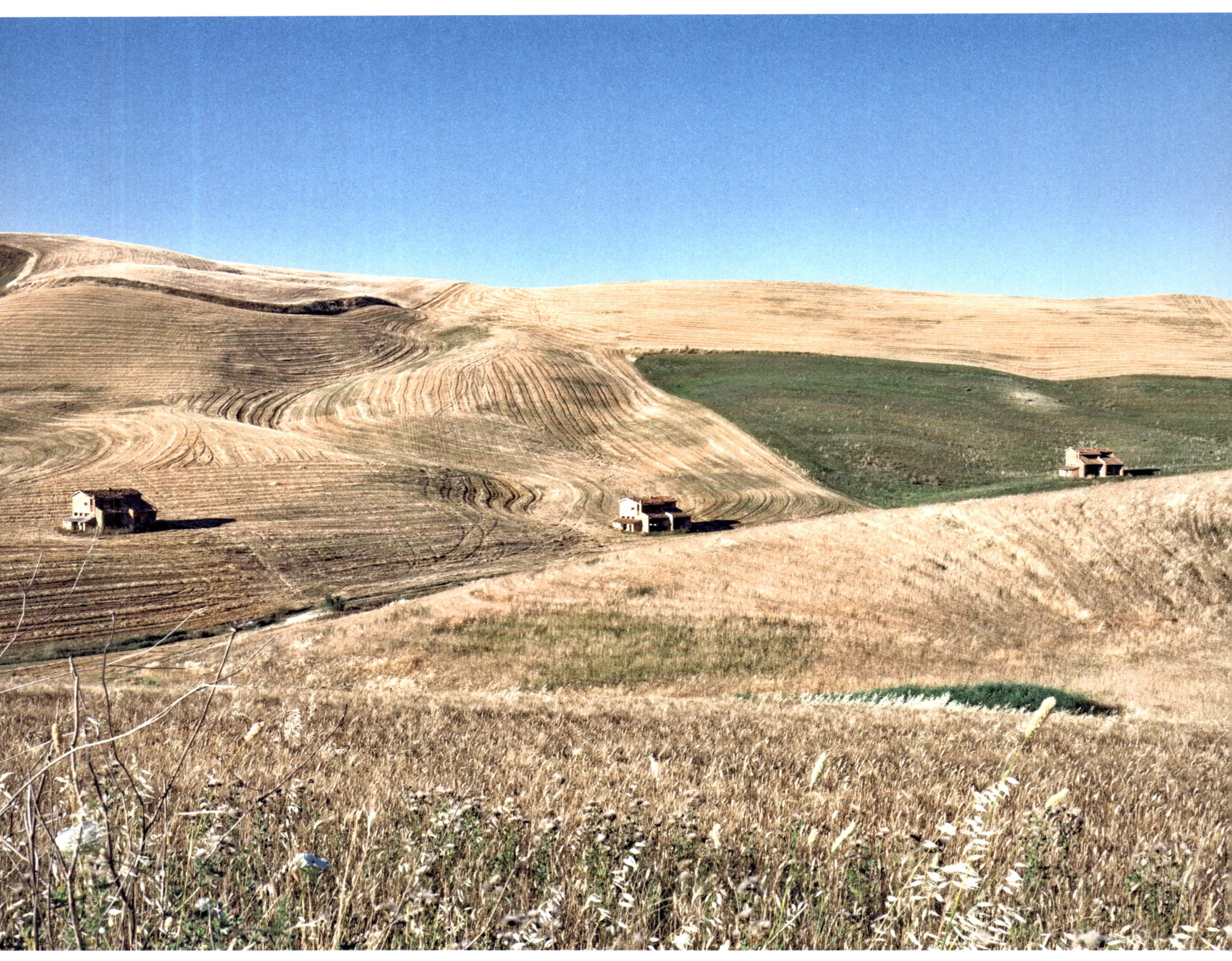

Figure 11

FABIO BENINCASA

Rubble of History and Sparkles of Stories
in Steven Seidenberg's Photos

Photography, like archaeology, deals with presences and absences. It makes evident what is missing and connects it to what is observable. Therefore, it seems appropriate that the visual investigation of this archaeology of the recent past, carried out through Steven Seidenberg's camera, is almost phantasmatic in the eyes of a contemporary observer.

In Southern Italy, land reform is a centuries-old issue. Despite all the promises from the Bourbons to Bonaparte and until the political unification of the peninsula in 1860, the problem remained unsolved. After the end of the Second World War, and following a long and violent struggle by the laboring class, the government decided to implement the *Riforma Fondiaria* in Basilicata; the operation was in many respects politically and economically anachronistic. The failure of small farms and the competition of the expanding industrialization triggered a massive emigration in the area, not only to Northern Italy, but also to Switzerland and Germany.

For the foreigner, and perhaps even more so for the Italian, the images of Seidenberg's Basilicata evoke an unknown, liminal Italy, outside the stereotype of the rustic idyll that dominates the (self) colonized imagination of the Italian landscape, perhaps the backdrop suitable for staging a science fiction apocalypse of rural civilization as Pier Paolo Pasolini might have imagined it.

The mysterious objects investigated by Seidenberg lie inert as idols of an expired religion in a territory made monotonous and motionless by the agricultural mode of production of big landowners. It is a rural archaeology strangely more unexpected than the industrial archaeology we are used to in our information society. Countryside, unlike the urban space, is assumed to be "natural," free, and empty; it is surprising to perceive it suddenly as abandoned and oppressive. The architectural and social relics of the *Riforma Fondiaria* stand out against an uncertain line on the border between ruin and rubble. If Anselm Kiefer, born in the devastation at the end of the Second World War, claimed to love ruins because they could be the starting point of something new, the photographer proposes here to interrogate these puzzling remains. Are they terminal rubble of a malformed modernization or evidence of a "pure, undated time," evoked by Marc Augé in his book on the ruins, *Le Temps en ruines* (Paris, Galilée, 2003)? The French anthropologist in this case would have no doubts, since he states that in our modern world rubble no longer has time to become ruins.

Yet in these images, the overwhelming skies, the steady light, and the flat impassiveness of the surrounding plain make the solitary walls specimens of monadic romantic ruins, at the same time suggesting indecipherable postmodern artifacts, out of place, existing on a borrowed time. The indefinity of their condition loads them with charm and ambiguity, but requires the photographer to make clear choices to transmit their essence in some way, to represent successfully the sense of their fecundity beyond the simple aesthetic pleasure.

The world "perfect," coming from Latin "perfectus," means completed, accomplished, in all its parts. In a sense, the charm of these modern ruins is their imperfection; they are not only the rest of what has been accomplished, but also evidence of what has never been finished.

Over the years, the artists of the Italian collective Alterazioni Video have notoriously paid great attention to the thousands of public works launched by the Italian State and never concluded. The Centro Internazionale di Fotografia in Palermo, directed by Letizia Battaglia, exhibited their photographic *Atlas of Unfinished Works in the Country*, aiming to identify incompleteness as the true Italian aesthetic style. In their "Manifesto of the Sicilian Incompletion," among other things, we read that the uncompleted style "musters and reassembles metaphysical places of contemplation thought and the imaginary....These are places of existential awareness, embodiments of the human soul, and they are silhouetted against the horizon testifying to our very nature as humans."

At first glance, Seidenberg's images of these abandoned spaces may relate to the perception of the incompletion in the Italian landscape. However, if Seidenberg's photographic gaze had stopped simply to verify this incompleteness, his artistic support to the archaeological and anthropological enterprise would have risked leaning towards mere symbolism. Walter Benjamin saw in the ruins the allegory of thought itself: "Allegories are, in the field of thought, what ruins are in that of things" and undoubtedly too many ruins have been depicted and photographed, over time, so as not to run the risk of triggering an unlimited chain of signifiers

Looking at the photos of the abandoned buildings, our attention initially focuses on an insistent internal-external relationship, lingering on doors and windows: openings that from dark interiors overlook brightly indifferent landscapes or on the stubborn resilience of the concrete walls to nature, inexorably tending to reabsorb them. The absolute lack of human figures in these images amplifies their metaphysical suspension.

So far, Seidenberg's meditation on the end of history and the incompleteness of human action either considered as an Italian style or, politically, as an inevitable fate dooming the optimism of postwar social policies. However, it is from his interest in the detail of the interiors, from his attention to natural data that we understand the possibility of investigating the daily objects as a slag of history and a spark of human stories.

The examination of the walls with their worn plasters, the expressionistic constellation of stains and debris, the destroyed furniture, still trying to evoke a mimetic domesticity, lead the viewer to be interested in the human beings who tried in vain to live their utopia according to the Kafkaesque bureaucracies of the *Riforma Fondiaria*. Their ghostly absence becomes a resonant presence in the abandoned spaces of the rooms, while the old broken cathode tubes allude to the irresistible call of an urban industrialism, a magic mirror that has sucked them towards emigration, towards a newly attractive utopia becoming equally illusory over time.

The graffiti covering the walls, the humble pallets, rags, food leftovers, and relics of small bonfires are also traces of transits, presences that have temporarily occupied the void left by the ghosts of the *Riforma Fondiaria*. In a sort of eternal recurrence, migrants and casual workers found a temporary shelter in these rubble-ruins without being able to stay, except for synecdoche.

Seidenberg's detached yet empathic gaze allows us to see the intertwining of dramatic and unfinished human stories, behind the mechanism of history and its curtain of incomprehensible debris. His tireless and trustful attempt to give a figural dimension to the void left by these stories is perhaps the most admirable characteristic of his inexhaustible artistic effort.

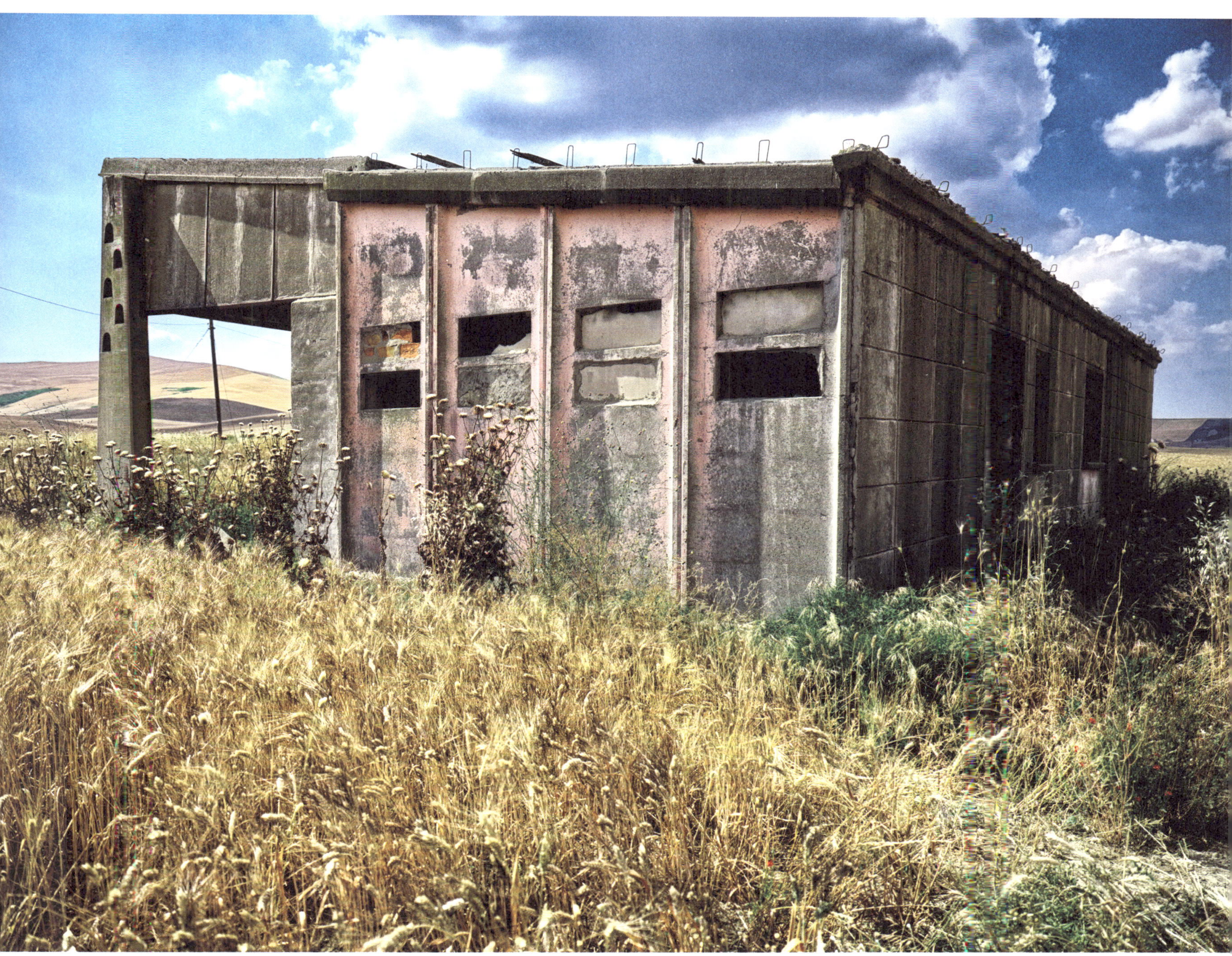

Figure 12

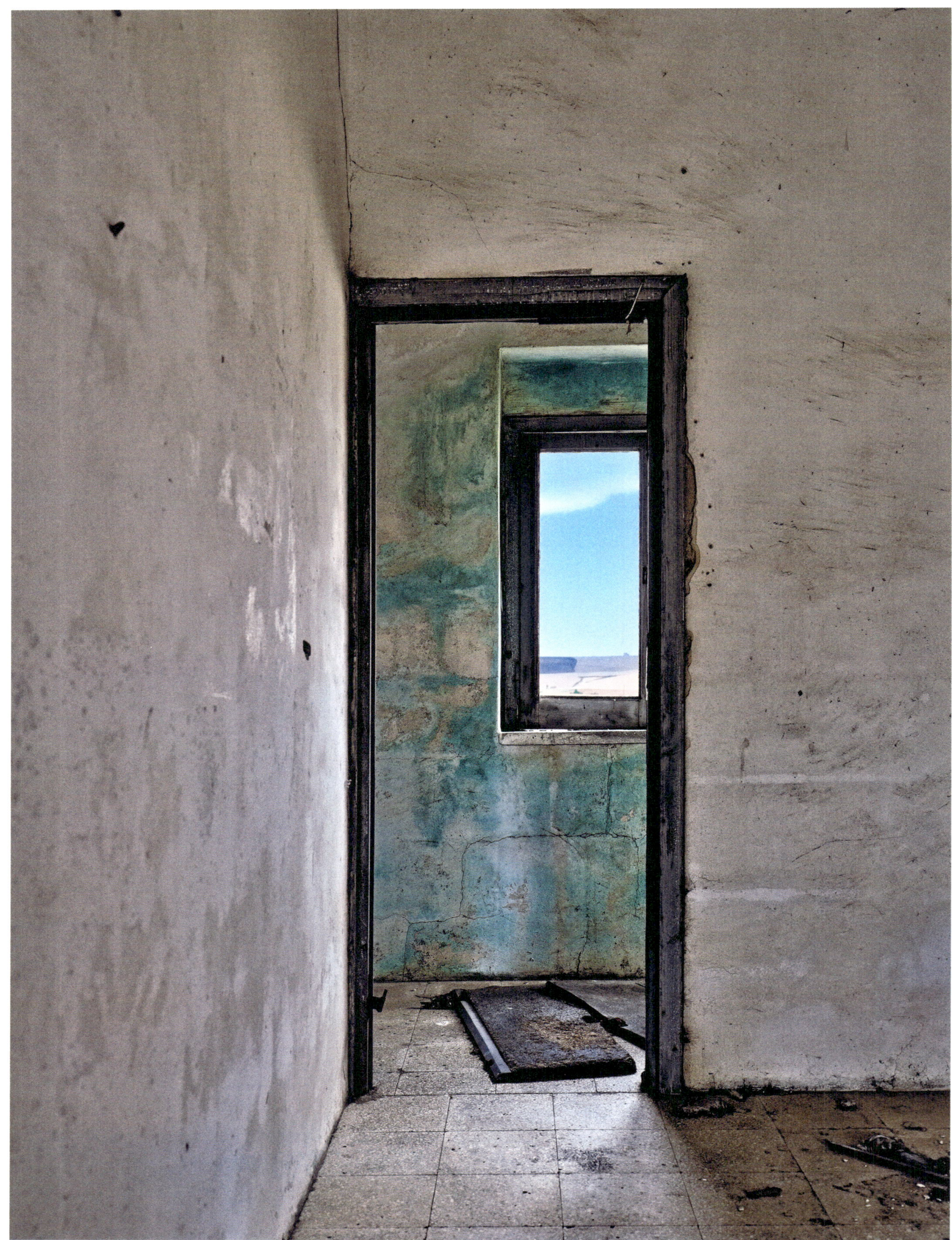

Figure 13

MAE LOSASSO

The Time Is Now

I began to unwind the thread of memory, discovering not only events of the past but the infinite, poetic contemporaneity of all time and every destiny.[1]

Something strange has happened to time in the Italian South. Cities hewn from rock persist in their existence, even though the last inhabitant left with the mass evacuation in 1952. Elsewhere, abandoned farmhouses dot golden fields, arms of wheat waving to these timeless forms. Vernacular architecture – architecture without architects – is archaic, that is to say, ancient – but it is also a beginning, as in *arkhē,* Greek for origin. These houses could have been built yesterday, or a hundred years ago, or 10,000; but no matter, because they are here, in the time of the now. Their existence is hard, material, and present. And if they exist in the contemporary, so, too, do they persist in the eternal.

The abandoned buildings of the Italian South are the material trace of its abandoned lives. The Italian writer Carlo Levi offered a sketch of these forsaken communities, in his 1945 book, *Christ Stopped at Eboli.* In 1935, Levi had been exiled to Lucania, the southern region known today as Basilicata, for anti-fascist activism. The book is the record of Levi's year in banishment. Yet it is also a work of recovery, an act of seeing, or of remembering, a part of Italy that had become a national *oubliette*; a forgotten place, as well as a place to consign those whom the state would rather forget. And it is here, Levi tells us, that Christ stopped, not to preach, but to turn back. The town of Eboli was the threshold, the point beyond which the Good News never travelled; lives abandoned, by God as well as state, a place out-of-time. "Christ never came this far," Levi writes, "nor did time, nor the individual soul, nor hope, nor the relation of cause to effect, nor reason, nor history."[2] Teleology has no meaning here; there is no beginning or end, only a perpetual, boundless present. Here, effect does not follow from cause and history does not gather, like the pleats of a dress, into something coherent.

1 C. Levi (trans. F. Frenaye), *Christ Stopped at Eboli* (London: Penguin Books, 2000), 5.
2 *Ibid,* 12.

Today, visitors to the Italian South might have a hard time under-standing Levi's relocation as a form of retribution. Basilicata, Puglia, Bari; these regions have become bourgeois holiday destinations, the abandoned farmhouses now melding with the landscape to complete the picture postcard. Matera–that city of caves, or *Sassi,* carved out of rock, first settled in the 10th millennium BC and con-tinuously inhabited until dismal living conditions forced the govern-ment to evacuate its inhabitants in 1952–was declared European Capital of Culture in 2019. Today, the *Sassi* are boutique hotels, museums, restaurants, and artists' studios; not so long ago, in the time of Levi's exile, they were malaria infested hovels, crammed with large families and livestock. Levi's description of the city is more evocative of Dante's inferno than a sun-drenched tourist hotspot: "In these dark holes with walls cut out of the earth I saw a few piec-es of miserable furniture, beds, and some ragged clothing hanging up to dry […] I have never in my life seen such a picture of poverty […] children with the wizened faces of old men, their bodies re-duced by starvation almost to skeletons."[3] So cities change, people migrate and arrive, old buildings decay and new ones spring up; yet still, in the Italian South, time remains suspended.

The work of Steven Seidenberg sheds new light on another moment in Italy's history, that of the *Riforma Fondiaria,* which, from 1950-1972, saw the reconstruction of the country's economy through a failed pro-gram of land redistribution and the building of new farmhouses. Only, as Seidenberg's photographs attest, these buildings do not belong to a discrete moment in time, because time here isn't segmented in that way. If the *Riforma* was out of sync with the needs of the Italian peo-ple, then it was in-step with the Italian South's timeless-contempora-neity. From one vantage point, these concrete structures have arrived from a time yet-to-come, like their Brutalist counterparts elsewhere in Europe. And yet, this is no Yugoslavian futurism, nor the utopian promise of Corbusian concrete. True to form, the farmhouses of the *Riforma* are simply another iteration of that ancient and eternal Italian vernacular. As in Levi's Lucania, these agricultural edifices are just

3   *Ibid,* 87.

more "scattered white houses, slightly pretentious in their poverty."[4] They are neither of the past, nor of the present, nor of the future. They belong, instead, to the contemporary.

"Contemporariness," wrote the Italian philosopher Giorgio Agamben, "is a singular relationship to one's own time, which adheres to it, and at the same time keeps a distance from it. More precisely, it is that relationship with time that adheres to it through a disjunction and an anachronism."[5] Agamben was born in Rome, that palimpsest of time, that tomb of faded history that is, also, always, timeless, infinite, eternal. It is a city that wears its ageing on its surface, while somehow remaining ageless, unsullied by the decay of ruin. Little wonder, then, that for Agamben, contemporariness is rooted in anachronism, in disjunction, and in archaism. "Contemporariness inscribes itself in the present," he writes, "by marking it above all as archaic."[6]

But to *be* contemporary; that is a matter of sight. As Agamben explains, "the contemporary is he who firmly holds his gaze on his own time so as to perceive not its light but rather its darkness. All eras, for those who experience contemporariness, are obscure."[7] The *Riforma* farmhouses, condemned to the *oubliette* of the South, exist in obscurity, in darkness. But the question remains: "What does it mean 'to see an obscurity', 'to perceive the darkness'?" For Agamben, the answer is to be found in the neuropsychology of vision. "Neuropsychologists tell us that the absence of light activates a series of peripheral cells in the retina called 'off-cells'," he writes. "When activated, these cells produce the particular kind of vision that we call darkness. Darkness is not, therefore, a privative notion (the simple realist of the absence of light, or something like nonvision) but rather the result of the activity of the 'off-cells', a product of our own retina."[8]

4 *Ibid,* 15.
5 G. Agamben (trans. D. Kishik & S. Pedatella), *Nudities,* (Stanford, CA: Stanford University Press, 2011), 11.
6 *Ibid,* 17.
7 *Ibid,* 13.
8 *Ibid.*

This is what Seidenberg's lens does in these contemporary land-scapes of the *Riforma Fondiaria*: it triggers those 'off-cells', transforming the darkness from nonvision to plain sight. Like Levi's text, these photographs betray an act of seeing. We are here, now, in the present, adjusting our eyes to the obscurity of the space, seeing the past, the *arkhē,* traced over walls, in a pattern of dirt, dust, and graffiti. "It is as if this invisible light," Agamben writes, "that is the darkness of the present cast its shadow on the past so that the past touched by this shadow, acquired the ability to respond to the darkness of the now."[9] To image failure is to see into darkness, and so to be truly contemporary. As Seidenberg writes, in his extended prose-poem *plain sight*, "Failure binds us to the present, inertia to the future."[10]

Plain sight is the textual accompaniment to Seidenberg's photographs of the *Riforma.* Like its subject matter, the poem is a work of "infinite deferral" (*PS*178), a stasis "empowered by stagnation" (*PS*10), which exists in a kind of temporal suspension, where "the look back is illumined by the mirror of futurity" (*PS*21). As we learn, in the poem's opening line, any possibility for forward momentum has been stalled, stifled by hyphenation and ellipses: "Shining rancor," Seidenberg writes, "the gall of the sky. From this moment forward—forsaken, delivered. Concede every breach but dissemble the void. From this moment forward…" (*PS*9).

Forsaken, like the abandoned lives and buildings of the Italian South, the poem becomes a palatial ruin, "a mustering of fragments" (*PS*9), that refuse to be shored. The relic of poetic metre can be heard, flying like Poe's Raven in moth-eaten trochaic octameter, in and out of the stanzas or the rooms, that crumble elliptically "as some discrete surrender to compulsory decay" (*PS*23). Or else, the ellipses at the end of every prose-block are the apertures, the doors and windows, onto which Seidenberg trains his lens in the gloom of the *Riforma* farmhouses. "Look there—the eaves are bearing down upon the

9   *Ibid,* 18-19.
10 S. Seidenberg, *plain sight,* (New York: Roof Books, 2020), 41. All subsequent quotations refer to this edition.

gutters. Turn round—the walls are crouching for the ambush, then the kill. What happened to the doorways? They were eaten by the moldings. Who's stolen all the windows? Perhaps they took their leave…" (*PS*72).

The poem is a screed, spat out through gritted teeth. It resides in the darkness. And yet, hope is not altogether abandoned; look hard, there amongst the rubble and decay. Seidenberg has given us, not light, but a way of seeing in the darkness, where dim traces of faith still linger, "as one believes that there is something else, that someday something more than what has happened…than what's happened into *happening right now* will cleave the darkness with the taint of new arrivals and so *save the coming day*…" (*PS*12). It's not what *has* happened but what *is happening now,* in the now of the contemporary, that matters. It's not what these houses were, nor what they'll be, but what they *are.* Seidenberg "clear[s] the world of its attachment to ruination" (*PS*123) by locating vision beyond the materiality of concrete. "There is progress," he assures us, "there is *aspect*, in the rending of the cerement, the promise of plain sight…" (*PS*11). Not *cement*, but *cerement*, the death shroud; not the empty tomb, but the mantle left behind. Romanticizing the ruin only prettifies poverty; it's life that is contemporary, that's now, that's in plain sight.

But why seek the living amongst the dead? Shaded from the glow of time and teleology, the darkness of the South keeps it lodged in the contemporary. "Formerly, each end held the promise of a new beginning," writes Seidenberg. "Now, the sky has opened, the erosion of the future is integral and—this blighted mound is all that's left, a Calvary surveyed…" (*PS*55). The myth has been shattered: there are no new beginnings in endings, the future erodes under and a sky that is a void, and Calvary is nothing more than a blighted mound. A stanza is a room, but it is also a stopping point—and Christ stopped at Eboli.

Yet perhaps, like Seidenberg's "project of elision" (*PS*198), such stopping marks not abandonment but release; the release from teleology, its apocalypse and judgement, and the possibility of stepping to one side, instead of forward. As Seidenberg writes: "To find one's place in history one must linger past its limit, one must step aside" (*PS*19). It is this lingering at the limit, this stopping, this unravelling, that marks, as Agamben writes, "the contemporariness with the Messiah, which [St Paul] calls precisely the 'time of the now' (*ho non kairos*). Not only is this time chronologically indeterminate," he continues, "but it also has the singular capacity of putting every instant of the past in direct relationship with itself."[11] When Levi arrived in Lucania, he, too, had to step outside of time to see into the obscurity of this contemporary Calvary. "I began to unwind the thread of memory," he writes, "discovering not only events of the past but the infinite, poetic contemporaneity of all time and every destiny." And in so doing, in this poetic act of seeing, Levi learns to look beyond the scattered buildings, to the *lives* of the Italian South. As he boards his train back to freedom, at the novel's close, he imagines that the sea is like "man's fate, cast for all eternity in a series of equal waves, moving through time without change. I thought with affectionate sorrow of the motionless time and the dark civilization I had left behind me."[12]

In 1964, Pier Paolo Pasolini returned to the abandoned city of Matera to make his biblical neorealist masterpiece, *The Gospel According to Matthew.* Among the cast, a young Giorgio Agamben appeared, playing Christ's disciple Phillip–discovering, perhaps, the meaning of Messianic time. But Pasolini, known as much for the profane as for the sacred, did not bring light to the Italian South, nor did he set time in forward motion. Rather, his film, like the landscapes his camera captures, and like the lives inscribed on the faces of his vernacular cast, remains a true gesture of the contemporary–then, as now, as fifty years from now. Just so, Seidenberg's *plain sight*–his photographs, and the larger project out of which they emerge–step to one side of history to find contemporary meaning in empty space. For "every empty space bespeaks

11 Agamben, *Nudities,* 18.
12 Levi, *Christ Stopped at Eboli,* 253.

the certainty of filling" (*PS*82); of filling, that is, with life—again and
again, in the time of the now.

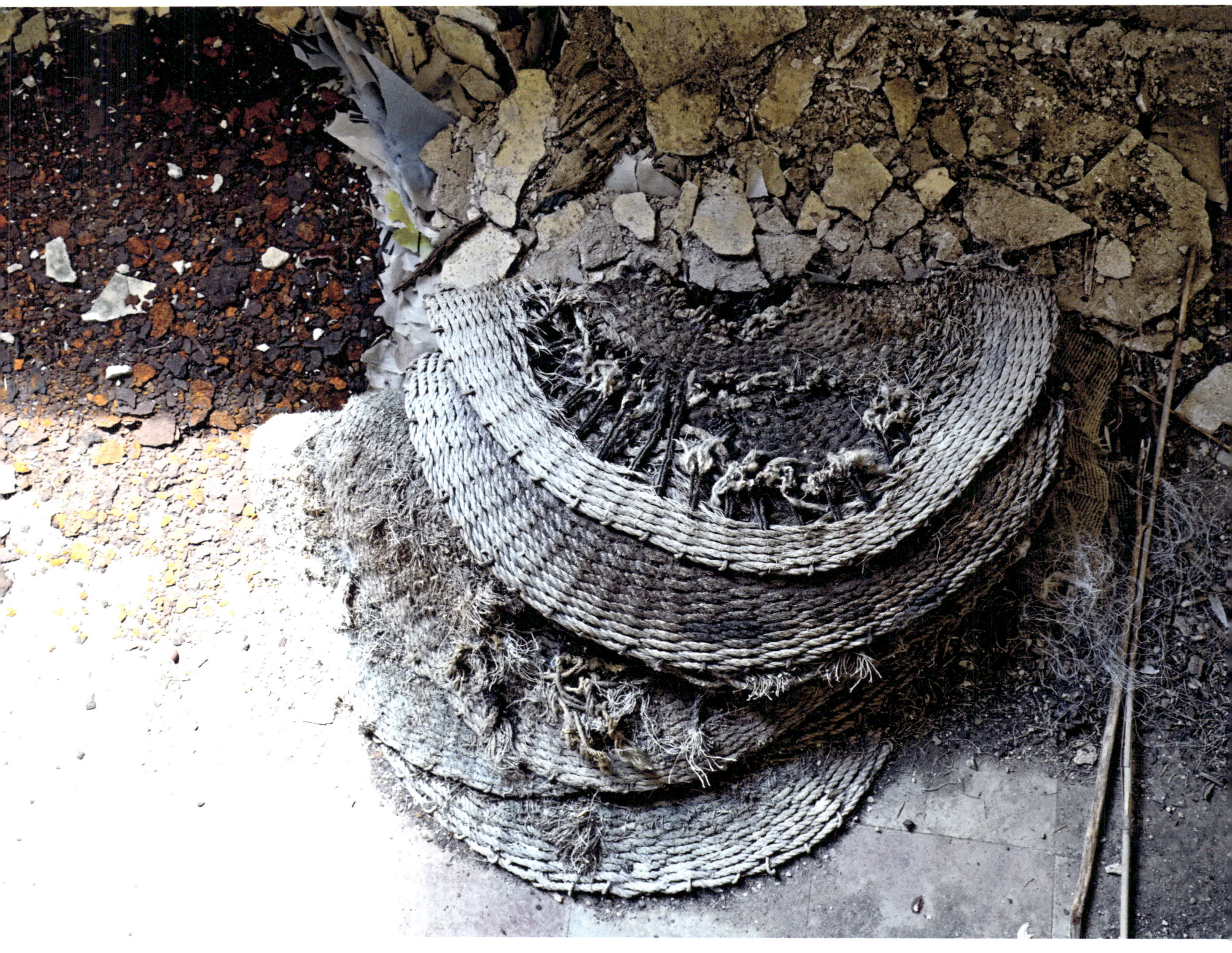

Figure 14

Landscape and the Italian Nation:
Rural Past and Present

Italy, during the chronological span of the *Riforma Fondiaria* project (1950-1972), saw a dramatic economic and societal transformation. Data on employment in agriculture shows that the Italian nation, since its late unification, saw a steady decline of the population working in the countryside: in 1871, figures put this at 58%. In 1951, they had already declined to 42%, despite the emphasis of the Fascist state on agriculture and propaganda efforts to encourage economic self-sufficiency (one can think of the so-called Battle of the Grain, waged by Mussolini since 1925). In the postwar period during the intense wave of industrialisation, which befits the moniker of economic miracle, the decline of the population employed in agriculture picked up pace: 29% in 1961 and 25% by 1965. By 1991, figures had fallen to 8.5%, and are now around 3.8%.[1] These figures show that Italy in the immediate postwar period was still predominantly a rural country, mostly pre-industrial, with pockets of industrialisation in the North West, but that at the time of the *Riforma Fondiaria* the pace of industrial growth and its associated urbanization was picking up sharply.

In many ways the *Riforma* was doomed to failure on macroeconomic grounds. Yet failure was also imbricated with long-standing prejudice and the discursive construction of the South as 'other' to the industrial, modern and modernised North. Related to this process were the real and perceived changes to Italy's countryside and its landscape, from populated to unpopulated, and the real and perceived role of cities and city living. Steven Seidenberg's photographs help us to look at the complex layers of representations of both Italy and its southern regions, as well as the postwar relationship between urban modernity and the perceived backwardness of rural areas.

The first time I met Seidenberg, at a conference I organised with Florian Mussgnug at the British School at Rome in the autumn of 2019, I was struck by his particular way of framing the subject; his way of seeing, to borrow John Berger's term. We were shown a series of

---

1   http://data.worldbank.org/indicator/SL.AGR.EMPL.ZS Accessed January 31, 2020.

images from the Roman squat of Metropolis and the community of Baobob that he had been documenting for an interdisciplinary project with Carolyn White. Seidenberg explained that his photographs never include people, yet the images we saw were deeply human, showing the palpable traces of the people that occupied the spaces, their vivid sense of style, the objects that they had chosen to surround themselves with, giving us clues to their everyday life and, more importantly, casting a light on the shared experience of our common humanity: the untidy shelf above a washbasin; the neat pile of clothing in the corner of a room; the flair for color and pattern on the wall or floor covering of some of the occupied spaces. Here was a photographic eye that was not intruding into these spaces, an eye that trod carefully and engaged with great respect in the lives of others.

In the series of photographs, Seidenberg allows us to reflect on the significance of the frame once more. In one, an open window frames golden fields, the faded mauve of the interior complementing the yellow of the ripe corn, brown patches of the fields in the mid-distance and pale blue sky on the horizon (Figure 9). What we see through the window is compositionally a classical landscape view, carefully proportioned and arranged.

This quintessential view of the Italian landscape is associated with the work of French landscape painter Claude Lorrain (born 1600, Chamagne, France—died Nov. 23, 1682, Rome [Italy]) who in many ways invented the classical Italian landscape that we still imagine today. The picturesque tradition was of seminal importance in creating an image of Italy in the European imagination as a land untouched by modernisation; the hold of this tradition became even stronger in the late eighteenth and nineteenth centuries in the face of widespread industrialisation in major European countries like Britain, France, and Germany, as well as in North America.

The most influential theorist on landscape painting, Pierre-Henri de Valenciennes, in his 1800 treatise *Reflections and Advice to a Student on Painting, Particularly on Landscape*, argued that there are two ways to see nature. The first is to see nature just 'as it is,' and to present it as faithfully as possible. In this case the artist selects a particular view because it seems more agreeable and picturesque. The second is to see nature "as it might be" and in order to do this the artist needs to be acquainted with the ancient and modern poets as well as being familiar with great painters. Valenciennes' ideas shaped profoundly the way artists approached landscape painting throughout the nineteenth century: the aim was to see nature through one's imagination which had been educated by reading ancient and modern poetry and by studying the work of other painters.

The landscape of Italy for painters, writers, and travellers alike, was more often than not perceived through the second way of seeing outlined by Valenciennes: the image of Italy, a country traditionally associated with beauty and the aesthetic, was seen "as it might be." The country was a living palimpsest that offered itself to the inspection of the foreign eye trained to see it through multiple lenses, producing complex views in which literary memories of the past combined with a repertoire of images (paintings, etchings, prints, and more recently photographic, televised, and digital images); these narratives and images shaped present and future memories of Italy.

Seidenberg's photographs give us a complex visual record of Italy "as it might have been" had the *Riforma Fondiaria* been a success, but they also hold a mirror up to the Italian nation about how the country and its countryside really was and is. This project is not journalistic reportage wearing its bias openly. What these images do is to capture the remains of the project and the layers of interaction with the houses and the land surrounding them over the past half a century.

In Figure 12 a passing cloud, creating a dramatically contrasted sky, casts a shadow that allows us momentarily to see the colors of the composition in their deep saturation: gold dotted with the green of a distant crop and weeds, the washed out grey of the cast cement structure, and the faded pink traces of the external rendering of the house. The interior of one of the properties seems to bear the traces of the optimism that these dwellings promised at the time of the *Riforma Fondiaria* (Figure 13). We see a rectangle of blue sky through a double frame: a doorframe and window, the carefully rendered walls of the rooms we are entering allowing us a glimpse of past modernity.

Within the series many of the photographs of the interiors capture fragments in abstract form. I am particularly drawn to these because they seem to function on multiple levels. They show us the important contribution of the intervention of creative practitioners and artists in interdisciplinary conceived projects—the way artists create a visual record is complementary to the work of archaeologists and heritage studies specialists. They make us look with a particular intensity at the traces of the past, at the way human habitation and the natural elements modify environments. They also have a particular resonance for me, a classically trained art historian, with a particular personal interest in non-figurative painting: color, form, and composition are the language I was trained to understand; in the images in this series these formal elements tell a compelling story through Seidenberg's ability to capture texture. In Figure 14, rubble in different colors is captured next to the remains of intricately woven material (a nest of baskets?); details of a shuttered window frame invite us to look up close at the grains of the wood and the basic construction of the shutter itself; in another image we see the faded cerulean blue of a shutter against a chequered red and grey tiled floor (Figure 15); in others we see discarded textiles on a dusty floor; Figure 16 frames a section of an internal wall that, palimpsest like, fades from dark moldy green to the soft powdery pink of natural plaster but, in one corner, it still bears the traces of a patch of cyan blue. Figure 7 is all about color and texture: the soft tall grasses lining the path, the clouds fading from dense dark grey to wisps of white against the blue sky; the textured stained concrete of the dwellings; the pockets of verdant weeds growing in the shade of the house in the middle distance, all create a harmony in golden ochre, soft greys and blue.

Norman Bryson reminds us that "the frame establishes a convention whereby art is marked as semantically mobile, changing according to its later circumstances and conditions of viewing."[2] Looking at the images in this volume, and listening to the critical and creative voices that have been asked to respond to Seidenberg's photographic works, I am struck again by this semantic mobility/instability, by the power of the image to enfold meaning within it only to unfold it again, offering multi-layered possible interpretations, every time responding anew to the challenge of reading the image, of thinking through its interpretive potential.

2   Norman Bryson, 'Introduction: Art and Intersubjectivity', in Mieke Bal, *Looking in. The Art of Viewing* (Amsterdam: G+B Arts, 2000), 3.

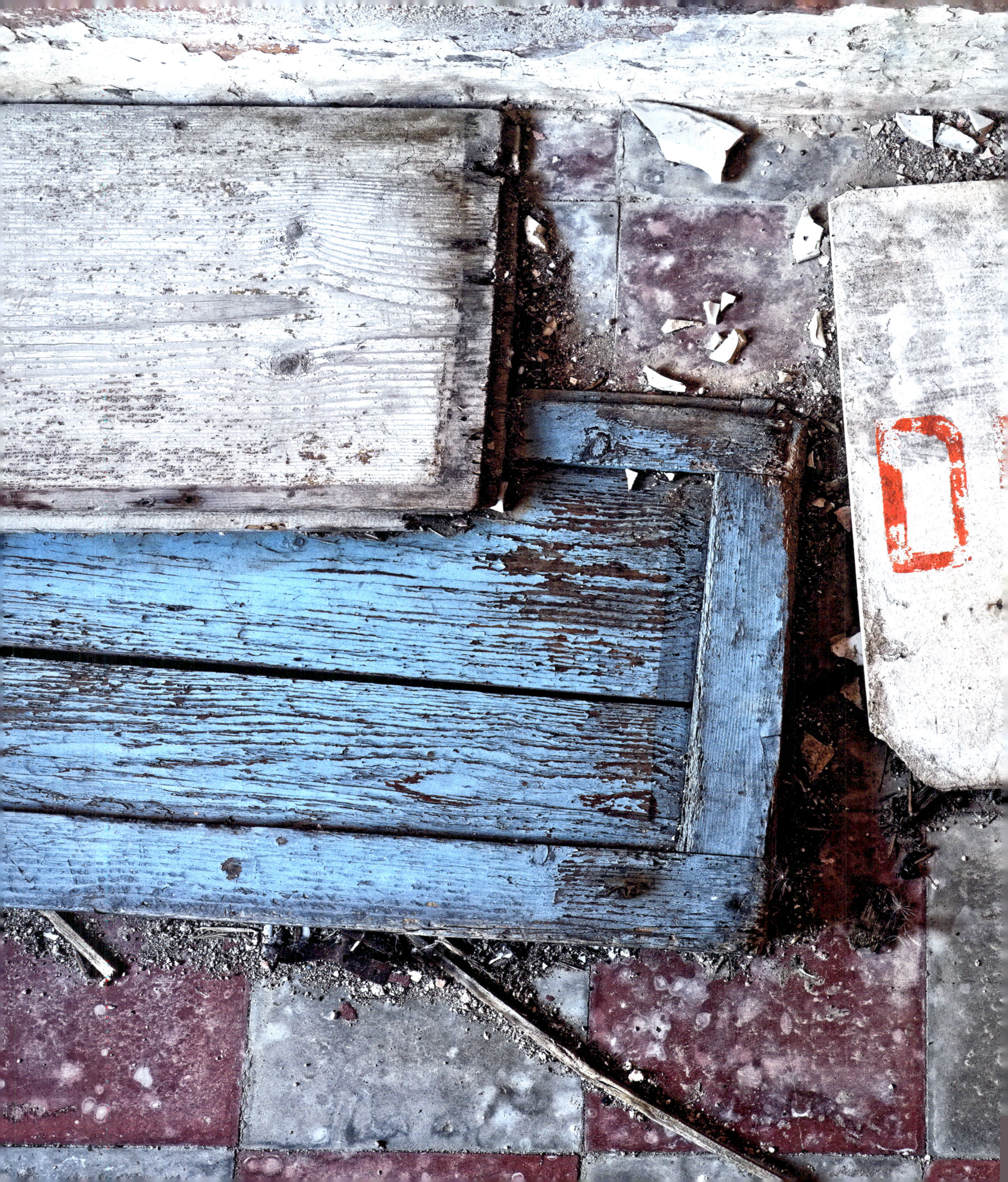

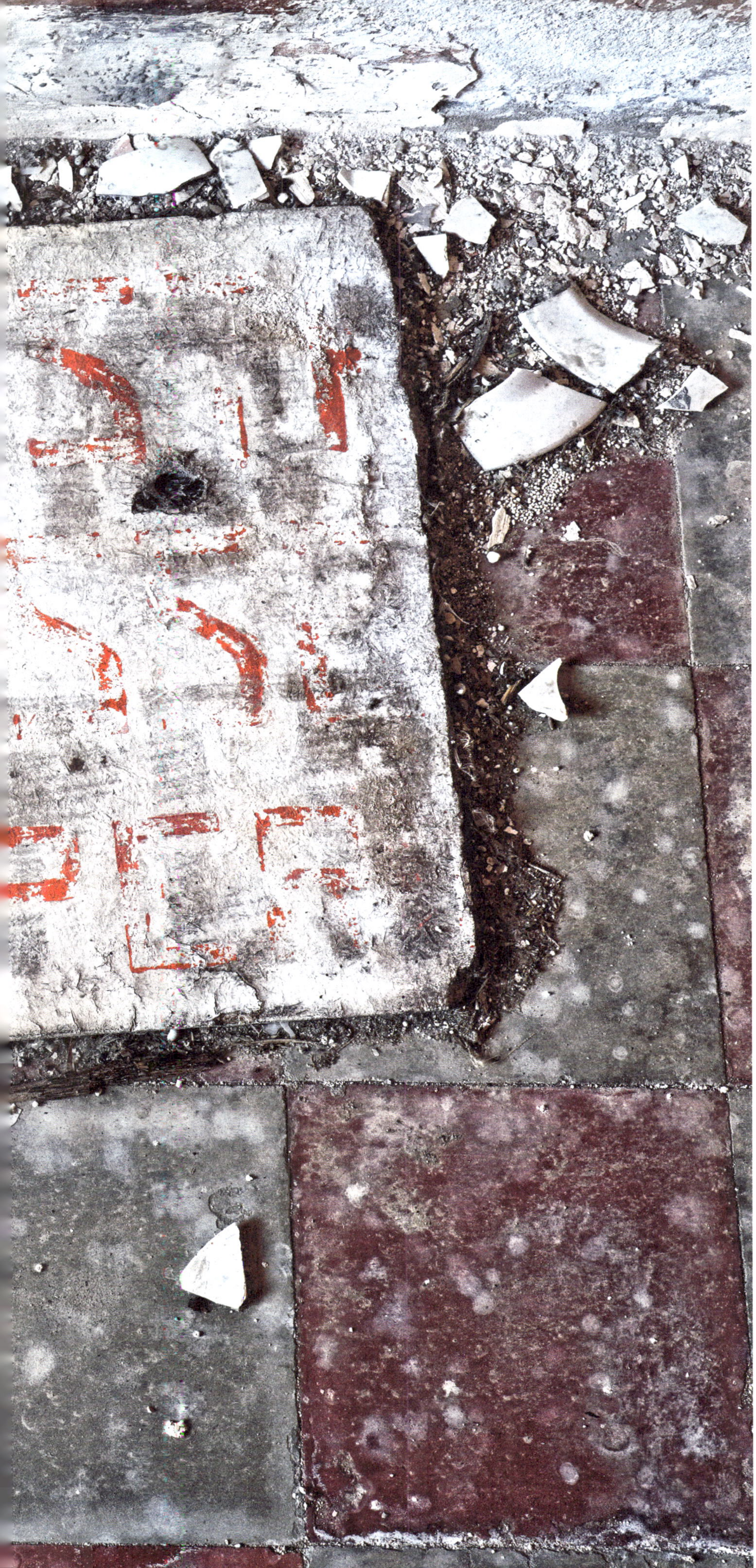

Figure 15

Brunella Antomarini teaches Aesthetics and Contemporary Philosophy at John Cabot University, Rome. She has a pluri-disciplinary formation in contemporary epistemology, aesthetics, anthropology, and post-humanism. A few recent publications: *Le macchine nubili* (Castelvecchi, Rome, 2020); *Haephestus Re-Loaded* (Punctum, LA, 2019, as co-author); *Thinking Through Error: The Moving Target of Knowledge* (Lexington Books, Lanham, 2012); *The Maiden Machine, Philosophy in the Age of the Unborn Woman* (Edgewise, New York, 2013).

Carmen Belmonte is an art historian specializing in modern and contemporary art. She is a research associate at the Kunsthistorisches Institut in Florenz, Max Planck Institute and a fellow of the Italian Academy for Advanced Studies at Columbia University, New York. Her research focuses on the visual culture and legacy of Italian colonialism and fascism and on cultural heritage in contemporary Italy.

Fabio Benincasa is a writer, editor, curator, and university lecturer. He is the editor of *Frontiere della Psicoanalisi,* a multidisciplinary journal. Between 2018 and 2019, he was Assistant Curator at MACRO Asilo. He currently teaches for Duquesne University Rome Campus and Università Niccolò Cusano.

Maria Teresa Carbone is a contributor to the cultural pages of the newspaper "il manifesto" and to various magazines on paper and online and she holds courses in journalism for the University of Roma Tre and the University of California Abroad Program. From 2014 to 2019 she coordinated the online literary review "Alfabeta2" and previously directed the Culture section of the weekly magazine "pagina99". Her latest books are *Che ci faccio qui? Scrittrici e scrittori nell'era della postfotografia* (Italo Svevo 2022) and the collection of poems *Calendiario* (Aragno 2020).

Jilke Golbach is Curator of Photographs at the Museum of London and a doctoral researcher in critical heritage studies at University College London. She previously worked as Assistant Curator at the Barbican Art Gallery in London, co-curating the exhibition 'Dorothea Lange: Politics of Seeing' (2018). Her research explores urban heritage, regeneration, and the 'right to the city' in relation to modern ruins in Rome.

Peter R. Kalb is the Cynthia L. and Theodore S. Berenson Chair of Contemporary Art at Brandeis University. He teaches and writes on 20th and 21st century art and photography and is the author of *Art Since 1980: Charting the Contemporary* (Pearson 2014). Kalb contributed to Seidenberg's *Pipevalve: Berlin* and is pleased to return to questions raised by his photography.

Mae Losasso is a writer and academic living and working in the UK. She is currently writing her first book, *Poetry, Architecture, and the New York School* (Palgrave Macmillan, 2023), which will explore the relationship between the work of the first-generation New York School poets and contemporaneous architectural theory and practice. Mae is the recipient of fellowships from Yale University and the Peggy Guggenheim Collection in Venice. Her academic research has appeared, or is forthcoming, in *Textual Practice*, *Paprika!*, *Italian Modern Art*, and *The Contemporary*. Mae is an Honorary Research Associate at Royal Holloway University of London.

Saverio Massaro is adjunct professor in Urban Regeneration at the University of Basilicata (Matera) and a member of Urban Experience non-profit association. He promotes urban regeneration strategies and coordinates participatory processes in Apulia Region as a civic designer, consultant for public institutions, and as the director of the non-profit organization Esperimenti Architettonici.

Myles McCallum is an Associate Professor and Chair of the Department of Modern Languages and Ancient Studies at Saint Mary's University in Canada. He is a Roman archaeologist who studies Roman villas, Italian urbanism, and archaeological ceramics. He was the director of the San Felice archaeological excavations and the Basentello Valley Archaeological Research Project, which led to his interest in the *Riforma Fondiaria* settlements examined in this volume. He is currently conducting archaeological research in the

Velino Valley of central Italy at the so-called Villa of Titus and Baths of Vespasian and is a Co-Editor of the journal *Mouseion*.

Tommaso Ottonieri is the author of prose texts, verses, and critical-essay works. He has published: in prose, *Dalle memorie di un piccolo ipertrofico* (1980), *Coniugativo* (1984), *Crema acida* (1997), *L'album crèmisi* (2000), *Le strade che portano al Fùcino* (2007); in verse, *Elegia Sanremese* (1998), *Contatto* (2002), *Geòdi* (2015); in critical-theory, *La plastica della lingua: stili in fuga lungo un'età costrema* (2000), as well as (in the identity of Tommaso Pomilio) numerous contributions on nineteenth and twentieth-century literary culture.

Giuliana Pieri is Executive Dean of the School of Humanities and Professor of Italian and the Visual Arts at Royal Holloway University of London. She has published widely on 19th and 20th-century visual culture, cultural history, and popular literature. Her research interests are comparative and interdisciplinary, especially the intersection of the verbal and the visual, and the role of Italian visual culture in the construction of Italian identity both in Italy and abroad.

Frances Richard is the author of *Gordon Matta-Clark: Physical Poetics* (2019), and co-author, with Jeffrey Kastner and Sina Najafi, of *Odd Lots: Revisiting Gordon Matta-Clark's "Fake Estates"* (2005); she is the editor of *I Stand in My Place With My Own Day Here: Site-Specific Art at The New School* (2019), and *Joan Jonas is on our mind*, a volume of essays on the artist (2017). Her books of poems include *Anarch.* (2012), *The Phonemes* (2012), and *See Through* (2003). She is senior editor at *Places* journal.

Antonio Riello is an artist who lives and works in London and in Bassano del Grappa, Italy. Since the beginning of his artistic career he has been fascinated by the paradoxes and controversial issues of the Italian way of life. His work has been exhibited internationally, including at the Museum of Art and Design, New York and Galleria Arte Moderna, Torino, Italy.

Colin Sterling is Assistant Professor of Memory and Museums at the University of Amsterdam. He teaches across heritage and memory, museum studies, and artistic research, and is a member of the Amsterdam School for Heritage, Memory and Material Culture. He is the author of *Heritage, Photography, and the Affective Past* (Routledge, 2020) and co-editor of *Deterritorializing the Future: Heritage in, of and after the Anthropocene* (Open Humanities Press, 2020). He is co-editor of the journal *Museums & Social Issues.*

Carolyn L. White is the Mamie Kleberg Professor of Anthropology and Historic Preservation at the University of Nevada, Reno, and is the director of the Anthropology Research Museum. Her most recent book is *The Archaeology of Burning Man: The Rise and Fall of Black Rock City* (University of New Mexico Press, 2020).

All images were taken in 2017 in the countryside of Basilicata and Puglia, between Matera, Gravina, and Altamura by Steven Seidenberg.

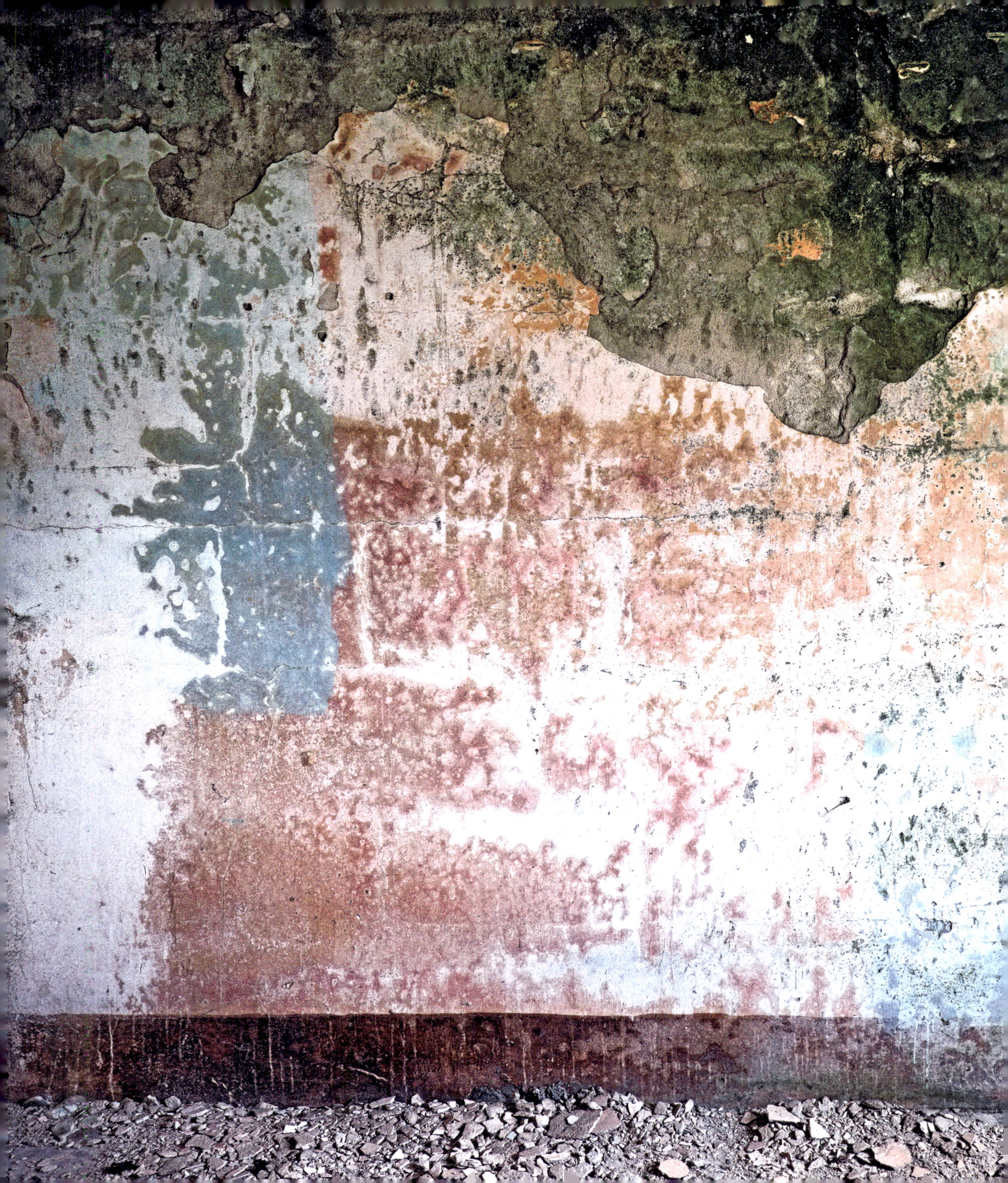

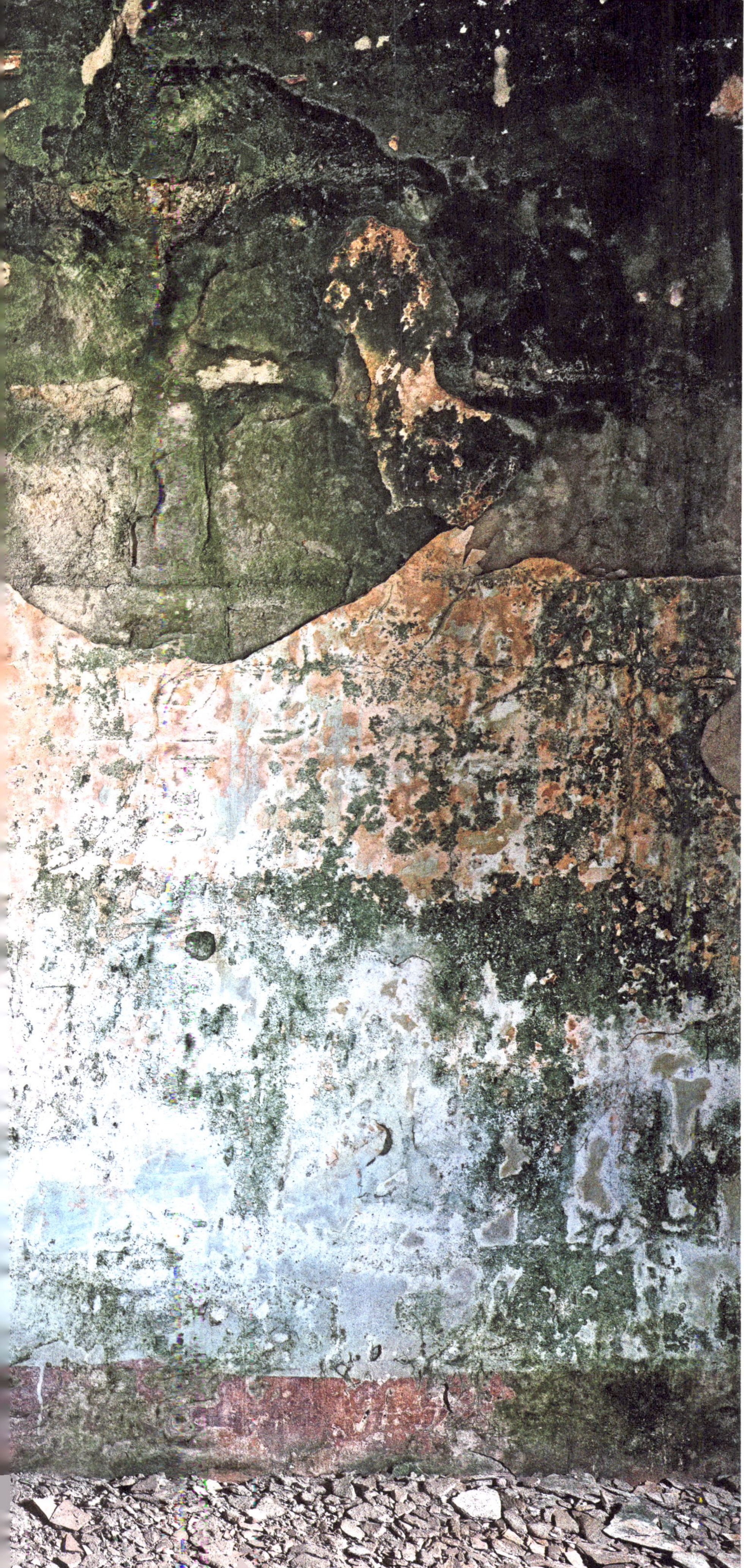

Figure 16